Dedication

I would like to dedicate this book to the memory of Muriel and Kenneth Lay, Peter's beloved Granny and Grandpa, without whom I probably wouldn't have survived to tell this tale!

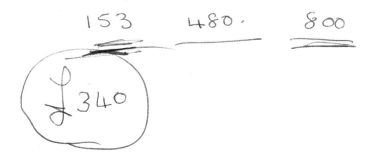

Acknowledgements

I would like to thank the many people who contributed to this book. Their excellent memories of events, sometimes long past, helped to bring together the story of Pete – his deeds and misdeeds – far better than I could ever have done, relying on my own brain.

Some are named in the book but I am not going to list everyone here, as it would be too long, but you will know which stories are yours.

My sister Janet gets a mention for the title, for which she was unwittingly responsible. I had been telling her a tale about Peter, regarding some bureaucratic mishap and at the end of it she exclaimed, 'Oh! For Pete's Sake!' I remember thinking, 'that would make a good title for my book' and from that point on, I knew I had to sit down and get on with it.

Hannah, my daughter, deserves thanks, not only for the assistance she has given me with the book but also for her endless patience with her brother.

Pauline Grogan and her staff at the John Gaffney Home need not thanks but a medal! Keep up the good work, Pauline.

My thanks also go to our families for their enduring support, our friends for making space in their lives for Pete and to all of the people who have given freely of their time to enrich Pete's life in some way.

For her advice and encouragement, I would like to thank my editor, Maureen Blundell and for his patience and generosity, my publisher, Peter Cooke.

To Andy – thank you for believing that I could actually write this story.

And last but not least, thanks to Pete, without whom there would have been no story to write!

If there are any errors in the book, they are most probably mine and I hope you will forgive them.

Yvonne Crabtree. Hellifield, Yorkshire, October 2007

Prologue

I pressed my throbbing head against the cool bathroom tiles and listened to the scream. It seemed to go on forever but I just stood there, listening. Eventually it stopped and I realised I'd been holding my breath. I still couldn't bring myself to move but I relaxed enough to breathe again, slowly. Then the awful thought occurred to me – perhaps she's dead. Perhaps he's killed her.

Hannah screamed again, shorter, shriller, and I knew I would have to intervene, even though the possibility that *I'd* be the one to commit murder seemed more likely with each passing moment. I envisaged the police arriving – a kindly policewoman comforting my daughter, the body of my son on the floor, me marched off to the police station and my husband, at work, being informed of what I'd done. Then, knowing that I could never put them through all that, I shook these fantasies away and went to rescue Hannah, once again, from her brother's clutches.

But I'm getting ahead of myself.

Part One

How it all began

May to December 1979, Sharjah, United Arab Emirates

I was lying on our G.P.'s couch at two o'clock in the morning having been unable to sleep because of agonising earache. Dr Arabi, a French-speaking Lebanese who spoke good English, inspected my ear and said, "I can't give you any pain-killers, Mrs Crabtree."

"But I must have something!" I wailed, in tears because of the terrible pain.

"You want to put your baby at risk?" Dr Arabi asked, and then beamed at me. "Yes! You're pregnant, Mrs Crabtree. I had your results today."

Momentarily lost for words, I found myself laughing and crying with absolute delight.

My husband Andrew and I had both been keen to have a baby but had delayed the decision because of our travels. Before coming to Sharjah we had spent two years in Zambia, then a year back in England where we bought a house, found jobs and fully intended to settle. However, after only about eight months we got itchy feet again and Andy began to apply for several jobs abroad, finally accepting an offer in Sharjah as Chief Accountant for Lamnalco, a marine supply company. We both quickly felt at home in the United Arab Emirates and saw no reason to postpone starting a family.

Andrew was also delighted at the news, and we were thrilled when Dr Arabi told us our baby was due on Christmas Day.

The pregnancy was an easy one – not too much in the way of morning sickness, no huge, uncomfortable 'bump' and very little unmerciful kicking; just a gentle fluttering sensation. I don't remember thinking there would be any specific problems during the pregnancy and birth, but I do remember having a very strong feeling that I should count all and any of these blessings.

We flew back to England at the end of July and spent a month visiting family and friends. I was very proud of my neat 'bump' and more than happy to wear the voluminous maternity clothes, which were very different from the clothes that expectant mums wear today. I did find, though, that in the early stages I couldn't bear any pressure on my tummy, not even the special maternity trousers with the unattractive elasticated panel at the front.

When we returned at the end of August, life was very relaxed in the Gulf sunshine. We lived in a town house on a small estate about three miles from the centre of Sharjah. Each house had its own small garden with access to the communal garden and swimming pool, which is where I'd probably picked up the ear infection.

Like many expectant mums, I was worried about tempting fate by amassing too much baby equipment too soon, but I gradually began to collect the basics: a navy blue carrycot on wheels, a wooden cot and a bath with a stand. All of these items were second hand and in very good condition but I still spent some happy hours cleaning and polishing them.

By the end of November, the nursery was just about ready and for the last month of my pregnancy, I spent my time by the pool in the late afternoon sunshine, when the temperature was at its most pleasant, with a cup of tea or a soft drink. I read the 'Guide To Looking After Baby' books that I'd bought in the U.K. and tried to imagine what my life would be like when I had a baby of my own to care for.

While in England I had really enjoyed helping to look after my two nephews, Andrew and Jamie, and my niece, Suzy. I loved the smell of newly bathed baby and the feel of a cuddly little body wrapped in a soft, fluffy towel. I couldn't wait to have one of my own.

When I woke on Saturday, December 8th at about five o'clock in the morning with a slight but persistent pain, I didn't take it to be the onset of labour as it was too soon. I lay for a while, waiting for the pain to go away, which it did after a couple of minutes. When it returned about twenty minutes later, I had a bath, then woke Andy and told him that I thought the baby was on its way.

We phoned Dr Arabi at about seven a.m., who told us to come to his surgery and greeted us with his usual offer of drinks – the strong, bitter, local coffee for Andy and orange juice for me – an offer hastily withdrawn when he realised I really was in labour.

With his usual reticence to examine me, probably because he was Muslim but still so strange in a doctor, he put his stethoscope to my tummy, assured me that all was well and said that we should go to the hospital.

The Rashid hospital was in Dubai, about twenty miles away. Arriving at the reception desk at about eleven in the morning, after a brief visit to Andy's office, we were dismayed to discover that the one thing I had forgotten to take with me was my hospital registration card. The receptionist was unwilling to admit me without it, I didn't want Andy to leave me in reception while he went back for it and I certainly didn't want to risk a forty-mile round trip. Panicking, we eventually hit on the idea of ringing a neighbour who had a key to our house, so that she could get the card and read them my registration number. All this took about half an hour and I was very relieved when I was finally given clearance to go through to the ward.

Strangely, up to then, the staff had been very happy for me to stand around in reception and hadn't been at all concerned that I might have to make the return trip to Sharjah - but once I'd been admitted, I had to make the short journey to the ward in a wheelchair!

As we were in a Muslim country, Andy was not allowed to be present at the birth. Despite the growing trend in the U.K. for fathers to be more involved, he was not overly keen on being there, anyway. I had thought that I was happy about this but now that the time had come, I really didn't want him to leave. The idea of having the baby abroad had seemed romantic - but now I just felt scared. I was given an internal examination (with Andy out of the room) and told that it would still be quite some time before the baby was born.

At about four o'clock in the afternoon, the staff told Andy that he should go home, as I was still no further into labour. He had, of course, only just left when things began to speed up and I was quickly moved to the labour ward. Poor Andy had only just arrived home when they phoned to tell him to return! Our son was born at half past six, weighing 6lb 13oz, with a full head of thick, black hair and everything seemingly fine.

The nurses put him into a cot by my side in the delivery suite and all I could do was gaze at him. I was exhausted but ecstatic. As I lay there, I recalled my Mum telling me that childbirth was 'the greatest pain in the world but the soonest forgotten'. When the porter came to take me back to my room an hour later, my baby was taken away to be cleaned up. Andy came in to see us but our son wasn't returned until nine-thirty and still hadn't been washed. We just assumed that the staff had been particularly busy, so began talking about names but then the staff shooed Andy away, saying that I needed to get some rest.

A doctor came in, looked at the baby and went out again; then later, a nurse suggested that I try to feed him. I had little success. I had wanted to breastfeed and assumed that the failure was due to my ineptness. The nurse was not particularly concerned and eventually took the baby off to the nursery, telling me to have a good night's sleep. I couldn't sleep a wink – I just wanted morning to arrive, so that I could be reunited with my son.

Breastfeeding still proved to be impossible in the morning, but the nurses didn't seem to be concerned and said that they would give him a bottle. I didn't feel that that was quite right but, as an inexperienced new mum, I bowed to their greater knowledge.

I was delighted when Andy came to visit later that morning and was able to hold his son for the first time. Immediately after visiting time, however, the paediatrician told me they were taking the baby to Special Care, as he had developed 'a bit of jaundice and a slight respiratory problem.' Again, nobody seemed unduly worried by this and, although I was anxious, I was reassured that this was very common and told not to worry.

Andy came back for the afternoon/evening visit and we went along to see the baby in the Special Care Unit. Andy was more vocal about his worries than I was at this stage, but the nurses were very quick to allay our fears.

By Tuesday evening, I was definitely more anxious. The baby was being fed through a tube and the nurses had given me a machine to express my breast milk, which they then threw down the sink. Still sore from the stitches, and feeling sad and slightly useless, I started to cry. I was in a strange country, had just given birth to my first child, with no family other than Andy around and almost no visitors. I suppose it was hardly surprising I was feeling weepy and a little sorry for myself.

One of the nurses in the SCU came over and asked what was wrong. I told her that I was very worried about my son. Unlike the others, who had been quick to reassure me that there was nothing to be concerned about, she smiled and said, "Don't worry, it's all in God's plan". Although I knew that she meant her words kindly, I didn't feel comforted by them but rather had a deep feeling of unease.

When Andy came to visit the next morning, we talked some more about names and decided that we would call the baby Stephen. Andy asked me if I knew how long we should expect Stephen to remain in Special Care and, when I couldn't give him an answer, he went to speak to the staff. He was gone for so long that my stomach began to churn and tie itself in knots. Eventually, unable to wait by myself any longer, I left my room and hobbled slowly and carefully down the corridor towards the nurses' station.

As soon as I saw Andy's face, I knew that there was something wrong.

The next few minutes will be imprinted on my memory forever. Andy held me tightly and told me there was a problem with our baby.

December 1979 to February 1981

The paediatrician, an Egyptian, spoke very good English and was very kind, passing me tissues as the tears ran down my face. I remember that he was suffering from a bad back and was wearing some kind of corset. He struggled to sit down to talk to us and then had to pull himself up afterwards, wincing with pain. I think the term 'Mongol' was used during his explanation but I can't recall much else that he said.

I do, however, remember him telling me that I should go home, as Stephen would need to remain in hospital for several more days.

I felt so low, especially after the excitement of giving birth. All our hopes and dreams for our new baby seemed to have been cruelly dashed: the baby that we'd planned for was not the one we'd been given. We felt cheated.

Over the next few days, we had to let our family, friends and neighbours know the sad news that our baby had Down's syndrome. That was a very difficult task, as we didn't really know very much about this condition and could give no real clue as to what to expect. We spent a lot of time in futile questioning – the usual 'Why us?' - as well as wondering if we were somehow at fault. With hindsight, I realise that ours was a common reaction of parents in this position - the feeling that we were responsible for his condition but at the time it was difficult not to feel guilty.

We returned each day to the Rashid hospital and each time I attempted to breastfeed Stephen, with little success. I was becoming very despondent - I felt that if I could breastfeed it would show that I was trying to do my best for him. The turning point, strangely, was when a nurse told me that, because of my baby's poor sucking reflex, it was very unlikely that I would be able to breastfeed at all and that I should stop bothering. Little did she know that was just the incentive I needed. I left the hospital that day absolutely determined that I would succeed.

We spoke to lots of doctors over those first few days who agreed that it would be a good idea for us to return to the U.K. to have our son checked over by a British paediatrician, as the occasional language difficulties made it frustrating for both sides. Through my eldest sister Val, we made an appointment with Professor Smithells at Leeds General Infirmary in January, and began to make arrangements to go home.

On the following Saturday morning, a week after our son's birth, we were told that we could take him home. Fortunately, the bag of baby clothes that I had originally taken into hospital with me was still in the car, so Andy dashed out to get it. Trying to dress our very floppy, sleepy son was a challenge. In the end I had to let one of the nurses help and we finally had him dressed and into the carrycot.

It had honestly never occurred to me that we could have left him for good in the hospital, although we were told later that some parents of babies with a genetic condition did just that. And there were times in later years, when things were desperate, when I did wonder if that is what we should have done. At the time, although I was very emotional and bitterly disappointed that Stephen wasn't a 'perfect' baby, I still felt very strongly that I had *wanted* a baby and I had a baby. He was just a bit more 'special' than other people's, needing more care and attention. Little did I realise then just how much more!

People were very kind, visiting us at home and bringing wonderful gifts for both Mum and baby (poor Dad missed out a bit, I think.) One kind friend, who had fairly recently had a baby herself, offered lots of practical assistance with the breastfeeding. We had discovered that baby Stephen could suck quite well on one breast but that when I turned him over to the other, he was unable to suck at all. With the help of a pillow, we found that he could actually lie on the same side, just further round, and was still able to suck. Feeding was slow but he was definitely making progress and I was glad that I had persevered.

Andy was wonderfully supportive during all of this, as well as trying to pop in to the office regularly to keep up with at least some of his work. He also said that he would register Stephen's birth and organise for him to be put on one of our passports.

When he arrived back after registering the birth, he looked a little sheepish. Sitting down, he looked across at me and said, hesitantly, ' I've got a confession to make. I didn't think he looked like a Steve, so I've registered him as Peter!'

Actually, changing his name to Peter was probably a good thing, as I can't imagine we would have come up with as many nicknames for Stephen as we have for Pete. Dr. Arabi started it off by referring to Pete as Poupee, the French word for doll. In later years, this transformed into Poopy, as Pete developed an alarming propensity to break wind, particularly after consuming beans or curry. Over the years he has been known as Peely, Perilous Pete, Pesky Pete, Pedro, Pierre, Pirate Pete and, for the past few years, Hairy Peter, as much in tribute to his interest in the Harry Potter films as because of his rather impressive beard and moustache.

Andy's Mum and Dad had flown over to stay with us, as planned, for two weeks over the Christmas period. After Peter's birth, I hadn't been sure that this was such a good idea but all the arrangements had been made and it would have been difficult to change all the plans at such short notice. In the end, we had a lovely time with them and we were very relieved by how they accepted Peter.

We went to a couple of parties over Christmas (with Pete in tow) and to the Lamnalco office dinner (leaving him with Grandma and Grandad). We had fairly quickly started to pick up the threads of life again, although I can remember very little detail of this period; I think I was on automatic pilot for a lot of it.

I found it very difficult to tell people about Pete's condition but I was quite happy to feed, change and bath him, all of which seemed to take an incredible amount of time each day. I was lucky that we had a young Indian man who came in three mornings each week to do the heavy housework, as I never seemed to have much time to spare in between dealing with Pete's needs.

Pete slept in his carrycot, at the foot of our bed for the first three months, so that I could hear him as soon as he stirred. He never cried when he woke and I was always afraid that he would not get enough to eat because he was so passive. I got into the habit (like many new mothers, I'm sure) of sleeping with one ear 'cocked', so that I wouldn't miss the small sounds he made when he awoke.

Feeding Pete took a long time. He would often fall asleep after only a few minutes sucking and I would have to nudge his cheek gently with my finger to rouse him. A feed that should have taken twenty minutes regularly took twice that time in the early days.

I was convinced that breast-feeding was the right thing to do but I was in agonies of doubt about the amount of milk he was getting. That, of course, would have been easier to evaluate had I bottle-fed him but having read that people with Down's syndrome were prone to gain weight, I really wanted to persevere.

Changing his nappy was also a slow job. He was very floppy and because of his lax pelvic muscles, his hips would splay outwards, making his nappies very difficult to pin securely in place.

Dressing him was even more of a nightmare. He wasn't uncooperative – it was just that his limbs were so relaxed. Pushing his arms and legs through the sleeves or legs of his clothing was frightening, as I was convinced that I would hurt him.

By the time I'd fed him, changed his nappy, washed and dressed him, it would be almost time to start the whole routine again.

As the paediatrician had suggested, we made our preparations for a trip to the U.K. With my sister Val's assistance we set up various appointments in Leeds and hoped that we would get a lot more information about Down's syndrome (or Mongolism as it was still sometimes called in those days). We had also joined the Down's Children's Association and had received some very useful information from them, in the form of several small booklets. Some dealt with practical aspects, such as feeding; others with the health problems that we might expect to face and some were personal stories, told by the parents of Down's children.

The health leaflets made agonising reading, as they seemed to be full of information about all the other problems from which Down's babies could suffer. At that time, I didn't even want to consider that there could be further disabilities.

We had booked our flights home in order to take Pete to see a variety of specialists, so I knew that we would have to face further ordeals, particularly as we had been warned that he had a suspected heart defect.

In dark moments, I really dreaded finding out that Pete had anything else wrong with him but I tried hard to present a positive, cheerful face to the world.

We flew into Heathrow and then took a tube to King's Cross Station to get a train to Bradford. By the time we were on the tube, Pete was obviously

15

hungry. He'd never had to wait so long for food before, so this was the very first time we heard him cry properly. It was actually a relief to hear that he could yell like a 'normal' baby, even though our fellow passengers probably didn't agree!

Andy's parents had offered to let us stay with them and we heard Pete exercise his lungs for the second time the very next morning. He woke up with a wet nappy and, being unused to cold weather, must have experienced a very uncomfortable sensation. He was certainly not going to put up with that and made sufficient noise to wake the whole household.

The next couple of weeks were a gruelling round of hospital visits, but we were also able to visit both our families, all of whom were very supportive. I think that because we'd had those first few weeks on our own, we had come to our own decisions about how we felt and how we would cope. So, when we presented Pete to our families, they were able to take their cue from us.

Of course we had done our share of weeping and gnashing of teeth but we had done it largely out of public view and were able to face the world with some degree of composure. We have always been grateful to our families for their complete acceptance of Pete, however much he has tried their patience over the years.

Although we hadn't attended church at all in Sharjah, I felt very strongly that I wanted Pete to be christened. We were able to have him baptised at St. Paul's church in Shipley, where Andy and I had been married. Val and our friend, Nick Denison, kindly agreed to be Pete's Godparents. Pete wore a lace gown that had been in Andy's family for several generations. He behaved beautifully throughout the service and at the small party held afterwards at my parents' house.

The trips to see the various doctors were a bit of a roller coaster, emotionally. Pete was found to have the typical type of Down's Syndrome, 'Trisomy 21'. This means that he has 47 chromosomes in his cells instead of the usual 46, the extra one being attached to the 21st pair. We also discovered that, in our case, the condition is not hereditary and that because of our ages when Pete was conceived, the chances of producing a baby with Down's Syndrome were about 2000 to one. With odds like that, perhaps we should play the lottery!

We also had confirmation that Pete had a small hole in his heart but the doctor was unable to tell us whether this would require an operation or not. Luckily, the hole has almost closed as Peter has grown and has rarely been cause for alarm. However, at the time, this was quite a concern to us.

It was during our visit to Killingbeck Hospital in Leeds to see this heart specialist that Pete vocalised his displeasure for the third time. Again, he was hungry and had been poked and prodded by various people all morning. A member of staff was trying to run some tests on him and, when Pete wouldn't stop crying, asked me a little frostily if I could give him a dummy. As he was generally such a quiet baby I hadn't seen the need for one but the nurse asked me if she could get one from the store cupboard.

Pete would have none of this strange item. After sucking like mad on the dummy to no avail, he spat it out so hard that it shot across the room and disappeared under a chair. I suppose we should have realised then that here was a man who would have a keen appetite and was not to be trifled with where food was concerned!

Having come to the end of our hospital visits, it was time to make the journey back to Sharjah. It was very difficult to leave the family but I must admit the British winter – cold, damp and dark – made the UAE seem like paradise. Once we had the results of all the tests we flew back to the Gulf and gradually began to get into some sort of routine.

Peter and I both started to attend physiotherapy sessions at the local hospital in Sharjah. On Saturdays, Mondays and Wednesdays we went together for sessions with a lovely lady, who hailed from Scotland. She showed us various exercises that I could do with Pete, to try to encourage him to support his own head and strengthen his back. She was remarkably helpful and gave me more confidence in handling him.

On the other three mornings (Friday being the day of rest, as we were in a Muslim country), I attended alone for physio on my back, which had given me quite a lot of pain during labour. During these sessions, I left Peter with my friend Pat Harvey, who was very supportive. Her young daughter, Caroline, enjoyed playing with Peter and he never seemed to mind how many toys she piled on top of him and didn't protest even when she occasionally tried to climb into the carrycot with him!

Support was also forthcoming from my next-door-neighbour, a nurse at the local hospital, who regularly helped me to put Pete through the exercise regime that I had been given to do with him.

I joined a mother and baby clinic, which was run by a British midwife in her own home, where the babies were weighed and there was an opportunity to talk about any problems. However, I still felt unable to talk openly about Pete's condition and as none of the other babies appeared to have any physical or mental defects, I felt like a real outsider and only went twice.

Our G.P., Dr. Arabi, attended Peter regularly and we also went to the Rashid Hospital in Dubai from time to time. Overall, Pete was making reasonable progress and was taking an interest in his surroundings. He had first smiled at about eight weeks old, while we were staying with my sister Janet in Scotland and it was, from then on, very easy to elicit a smile or a chuckle from him. He was a pleasant, happy baby, who still rarely cried. We knew that when he did, there really was something the matter.

In April, when the weather became warm enough, we started to take Pete into the swimming pool, which he instantly liked. He was completely relaxed in the water - so much so, that it was sometimes difficult to get him to move! When he began to weigh more and to move about more, we tried him with a variety of armbands and rubber rings, without much success. They were all too big for him and, because he was so floppy and loose-limbed, he just sort of slithered through the arm and leg holes. However, he never minded when he occasionally ended up with his face in the water and would just blink and shake his head. In the end, we found that a combination of armbands and rubber ring worked best, even though they made him look a bit like the Michelin Man.

The warm weather suited Pete and he definitely benefited from the climate, being generally free of the chest infections, colds and coughs to which many babies with Down's Syndrome are particularly prone.

Around this time we bought him a chair, which converted into both a high chair and a swing, which he loved. We also bought a baby-walker that had a fixed tray on the front. At first he used to flop forwards but eventually learnt to sit up so that his hands were free to play with the toys on the tray. I think he enjoyed the change of position and the fact that he could see the room from a different perspective. We also had a 'Bonny Bouncer' but we didn't use that much during this period as Pete looked rather like a drunken parachutist in it, hanging limply instead of bouncing up and down.

As Peter was very floppy, bath time was always interesting. It was difficult to hold on to him when he was wet and slippery. Eventually, I transferred him from the baby bath into the big bath. I found that, by putting him in just a couple of inches of water he could lie on his tummy and keep his head and neck out of the water. This left me with two free hands to wash him and gave my back a rest. **(Plate 1)** Once he had learnt to roll, he would turn over repeatedly in the bath, generally enjoying himself.

By the time we returned to England in July for Andy's annual leave, we were more relaxed with Pete. He was sleeping through the night, taking a limited variety but reasonable amount of solid food along with breast milk, and was definitely developing his own personality. Although he was nearly always good-humoured at this stage, he did sometimes show another side to his character that made us almost think he was a different baby.

Sometimes, we parted his hair in the centre and referred to him as Baby Cedric, Pete's imaginary Australian cousin. I have no idea why we chose the name Cedric, except that the hairstyle gave him a rather old-fashioned look, but I do remember that we did this when he was behaving in a particular way.

18

For brief moments, he would press his lips together and shake his head from side to side, very fast, as if he was really displeased about something and no amount of coaxing would make him stop.

Pete was amazingly good at adapting to new surroundings in his early days and responded very happily to all the friends and relatives who came and went in his life. The only times he showed signs of distress were when people shouted or raised their voices for any reason – not necessarily because they were cross.

We stayed in the U.K. for a month during the summer, away from the worst of the heat and high humidity of the Gulf. During this visit we were given board and lodging by my Mum and step-dad, who were both keen to be involved with Pete, playing with him, singing to him and generally helping to stimulate him. Pete loved music of any kind from a very early stage and would jig about enthusiastically to even the most tuneless singing, which was just as well as his Gran was pretty nearly tone-deaf.

We had another round of hospital trips, which I still found difficult. Although we were coping well with Pete on a day-to-day basis, we were both still very anxious about his future. I wanted someone to say that he would be one of the lucky Down's children who would be able to talk, walk, read and write and generally get through life without too much difficulty. Of course, no one was ever able to say that to us, as there's no way of telling how any child will develop, let alone a child with a mental handicap. We were advised to give him as much attention as possible and to keep him stimulated, in the hope that this would help his future development.

Professor Smithells noticed Pete's squint during our visit to him and also told us that Pete's testicles had not descended, but treatment of both conditions was deferred. Dr. Scott, the heart specialist, was the most enthusiastic about Pete's development and his condition. Tests showed that the hole in his heart had not enlarged and Dr. Scott was cautiously optimistic that he would not need an operation.

The general opinion of virtually all the medical staff we saw, both in England and Sharjah, was that we should have another baby as soon as possible. I wasn't really sure about this as I was, on one level, very content with my baby. He would put up with endless amounts of cuddling and attention but didn't cry if I put him down to attend to something else. He smiled and gurgled at the drop of a hat and didn't put up a struggle when he was being bathed, changed or dressed. Obviously, underlying all this was my worry about how he would develop, but I couldn't really see how having another baby would change that.

In the end, we decided to let nature take its course and, as I was still breastfeeding, we didn't think that anything would happen too quickly.

However, we had only been back in Sharjah for a few weeks after our summer break when I began to think that I might be pregnant again. I saw the gynaecologist towards the end of October, who put me at about 16 weeks' pregnant and told me that I should return to the U.K. for an amniocentesis test. She was not keen to carry it out herself as it was a relatively new procedure and I had had a small amount of bleeding. She said that it would be better if I had it done in the U.K., where someone more familiar with the technique could perform it and there would be less chance of causing a miscarriage, which was a significant risk even without the bleeding.

Arriving back in England in late October, I was admitted to hospital within days, as by this time I was starting to bleed more heavily. Andy and Pete once again stayed with my Mum and step-dad and came to visit me every day at the hospital. Performing the amniocentesis was out of the question now and I was confined to bed. After a month of this and no sign of any improvement, Andy reluctantly told me that he would have to return to Sharjah, as he obviously still had a job to do and his boss had been more than fair about the amount of time he had taken off work.

My Mum very kindly agreed to look after Pete and gave up her part-time job to care for him. I was allowed home at one point as things seemed to have settled down, but within a couple of days I was rushed back in by ambulance. I spent time in three different hospitals and began to feel increasingly desperate.

Pete spent his first birthday with Gran and Grandpa (as we called my parents – Andy's were Grandma and Grandad) with his Dad still in Sharjah. He was brought to see me in hospital and we opened his presents together and had a birthday cake. The nurses were lovely and all gathered round to sing 'Happy Birthday' to him but I was heartbroken after Pete had gone. He had begun to realise that when his coat was put on it was time to leave and he would start to cry.

Christmas must have been very hard for my parents, as by then I was in a different hospital, which had very strict and inconvenient visiting hours. These didn't fit in well with Pete's routine.

Immediately after Christmas, I was moved to yet another hospital. I was still threatening to miscarry and had begun to have contractions. The day before New Year's Eve, the gynaecologist came to see me and told me that neither the baby nor I was doing well. Her strong recommendation was that I should have the baby aborted, preferably within the next twenty-four hours. I was allowed to telephone Andy, who agreed to come home to be with me. He managed to get a flight on New Year's Eve and arrived at the hospital at about ten o'clock in the morning on New Year's Day, 1981.

I was immediately put on a drip to speed up the contractions and delivered Pete's brother or sister that evening. We were not allowed to hold or see the baby and I left hospital the next day without even knowing its gender. Nowadays, a baby born at 25 or 26 weeks would have some sort of chance but back then, it was never expected to survive.

As soon as I was pronounced fit to travel, we went back to Sharjah. I was at a very low ebb but pleased to be reunited with Andy and Peter. The warm sunshine was welcome after the dull January weather and I slowly started to come round.

Part Two

The Early Years

Return to England

While we had been in the U.K. back in the summer, I had been looking into educational matters for Pete and was becoming concerned about his schooling. Health care in Sharjah was fine but I knew there was a lack of educational facilities for children with any sort of handicap. I did read about one special school in Dubai but could never get any reply when I telephoned and I assumed it was no longer in existence.

At just the same time new people moved in next door, Marilyn and Richard Penneck, with their two boys. Marilyn introduced herself to us very soon after moving in and, incredibly, turned out to be the headmistress of the special school in Dubai.

She was so helpful to us, introducing us to the 'Portage Scheme', a new idea that was really for professional use. We were able to get a copy of this book through the headmaster of the school where Andy's Mum worked. I found it helpful in the way that it broke down lots of everyday tasks that Peter would need to be able to do (such as dressing himself) into manageable portions and explained, in clear detail, how to teach each part of the task.

Marilyn had a very positive attitude and helped to make me feel more hopeful about the future. She did say, however, that we should not rely on a place at her school being available for Pete, as she relied upon the local sheiks for charitable donations. This meant that she did not have financial freedom and could not guarantee the school's long-term future.

This information was probably what finally decided us to pack up and come back home for good, as there was nothing else in the pipeline for Peter at that time with regard to his education.

Pete was, once again, very well behaved on the flight and was becoming quite a seasoned traveller, having flown nearly 50,000 miles by this time. He had, in fact, been enrolled as a member of the British Airways' Junior Jet Club before his first birthday.

When we arrived back in England we stayed with my parents for a week until our house in Bingley, which we had rented out, was vacant. Pete, unsurprisingly, was very clingy, although he enjoyed the attention of his grandparents.

As his routine was completely thrown out by all these changes, he found it very difficult to get into a regular sleeping pattern. Everyone suffered from this, as he could only be put down in his cot after he had fallen asleep in someone's arms.

Moving back into our own house, which was unfamiliar to Peter, was yet another change for him to cope with. But he did settle down over the next few weeks and enjoyed zooming up and down the long kitchen and hallway in his baby-walker. He also discovered the washing machine and tumble dryer and would park himself in front of them when they were switched on and watch them for ages, an interest that has never dwindled.

Once we had established a routine, Pete did start to make more noticeable progress, learning to crawl by pulling himself along the floor like a commando, using the arm-over-arm method. It always looked hard work to me but he seemed to get around without too much trouble and enjoyed being able to get to his own toys and books. He still loved singing nursery rhymes and was making efforts to join in with both words and actions. He also learnt to blow kisses and enjoyed all the praise he received for any of his achievements, repeating them endlessly.

We hadn't managed to solve the problem of getting Pete to bed at night without him having dropped off to sleep first. Eventually the health visitor suggested that we should put him to bed and just leave him to cry, however long it went on. The first night, Peter cried for nearly two hours, by which time I was in tears as well. However, we stuck it out and eventually he did fall asleep. The next night he cried for a slightly shorter time and within a week or two was only giving a five-minute grizzle, as a sort of token protest. I am so glad that we didn't give in, because once Pete had settled into this new bedtime routine we rarely had any more problems about getting him into bed.

Another problem that crept in at around this time was that Pete started biting – usually my ankles or any other bare flesh he could find. Having had no teeth at all until he was thirteen months old, I can only assume that it was the novelty of actually being able to bite that made him do it. He would cry when I told him off but would still have another sneaky bite later.

On one memorable occasion, we were visiting Grandma and Grandad (Andy's parents) at their caravan. It was a lovely warm day and Grandad was lying outside on a blanket, sunbathing, without a shirt. Pete must have spotted the expanse of bare flesh and obviously just couldn't resist sinking his little teeth into it. I don't think Grandad had ever moved so fast before!

We were put in touch with MENCAP (then known as the National Society for Mentally Handicapped Children) and we also started to attend a playgroup for children with special needs and a Toy Library, both of which were in Keighley. We were also introduced to our first carers on the 'Give Mum a Break' scheme, although at the time we didn't think we would make much use of this, as we felt that Pete was too young to be left with people who weren't either family or friends.

At the playgroup, Pete didn't join in well with the other children and seemed not to like noise very much. I put it down to him being used to being at home with me for most of the time. Over the next few visits, he gradually began to relax and enjoyed the singing at the end of each session. I found the sessions useful, as I was able to chat with other mums of Down's syndrome children. I began to feel less isolated but was concerned that he didn't seem as confident as the other children and became anxious if I was out of his sight at all.

We were still doing the rounds of specialists at Leeds General Infirmary and Killingbeck and to that was added weekly physiotherapy and speech therapy, both of which greatly helped Pete's progress. He was slow to walk unaided but could now toddle round the furniture. His language was developing well and he was able to communicate with us, 'more!' being a favourite word. He would usually reply 'toast' when I asked him what he would like for breakfast but occasionally would surprise me by demanding 'cake' or 'chips'.

Surprisingly, in view of Pete's already developed interest in food, he was often very silly at meal times, throwing both spoon and food on the floor. He could feed himself with some assistance, as long as the food was chopped up for him, but it was always a bit of a battle. We had to watch his weight, as he was showing the common tendency of Down's children of being on the plump side. However, once he became more mobile, it was less of a problem and we were all thrilled when he eventually took his first steps unaided. (2)

As I have mentioned, we had been introduced to the 'Give Mum a Break' scheme and our neighbour, Denise Rankin, very kindly agreed to register as a carer on the scheme. Pete was happy to go to Denise's house or for her to sit in with him at our house and I felt comfortable with either arrangement.

One day, after Peter had been to stay with her for a couple of hours, Denise discovered that her washing machine was not working. After a brief examination, she called out the engineer, only to discover that the child lock had been activated. You've guessed the culprit, of course.

Having struggled to teach Pete to release anything from his grasp, we then went to the opposite extreme, where he just loved to throw - another pastime that has carried through to the present day. We tried everything to curb this anti-social habit, without much success. Even now, if he is bored or in a bad mood, he will throw things out of the window or at the light bulbs, all the while telling himself off for doing it!

Starting School

We started to look at schools in January 1982. At that time, the recommended school for children with Down's Syndrome was Branshaw View, in Keighley, a school for severely 'educationally sub-normal' children. Although the staff were very welcoming and friendly, I just didn't feel that it was the right place for Pete. I eventually gained a part-time place for him on a trial basis at Greenfield School for children with moderate learning difficulties.

After Easter, at the age of two years and four months, Pete started in the nursery for two mornings a week and settled very well, gradually increasing his hours there until he eventually went full-time in September, although still on a trial basis. Knowing how challenging he could be, I was always on tenterhooks, wondering if he would be expelled.

Transport to and from school was not provided for Pete at that time, so I had to take him myself. Andy worked in Harrogate then and although Pete's start time of 9.30am wasn't particularly convenient, he would occasionally help out by taking Pete to school for me. One day, Andy set off to drop Pete at school but with his mind presumably already on work, forgot to turn off to Greenfield. He had reached Otley before a little noise from the back alerted him to the fact that Pete was still there. Pete would have known that Andy had missed the turning, even at that young age, but was obviously enjoying the extra long ride in the car.

<u>Independence</u>

Peter's second and third birthdays were celebrated at home, with most of his relatives in attendance, as I suppose I was trying to make up for his miserable first birthday. On the evening of his third birthday, with most of our guests still enjoying the party, I suddenly realised that Pete had disappeared.

Slipping instantly into panic mode but not wanting to alarm our guests, I quietly told Andy my fears. We did a sweep of the downstairs rooms, checking that both external doors were still locked Then we moved upstairs, where we eventually discovered him, in his pyjamas, fast asleep in bed where he had taken himself without a word to anyone, having presumably had enough of being polite.

He favoured a fairly set bedtime routine as a rule, wanting to have several stories read to him. This was fine by me, as we both enjoyed this quiet time. When the stories were finished, he would lie in bed with his arms outstretched and I had to line up all his soft toys so that their heads rested on his arms, first kissing each one in turn and then holding it to Pete's puckered lips. Having gone through this rigmarole, he would then throw each one on the floor, saying 'Poor Teddy, poor Humpty', etcetera!

During this time, we had been trying to train Pete to use the potty. He picked up the idea very quickly and was soon asking to use it but he still needed nappies at night, despite us lifting him out to use the potty when we went up to bed.

We'd noticed that, since starting school, he was becoming more confident socially but less obedient and he needed close watching to prevent him from doing mischief. When we were out, if he didn't want to go in the direction we were taking, he would just sit down and the only thing to be done was to pick him up and carry him. This wasn't too bad when he was two or three years old but became quite a problem as he became older and heavier.

One of the things he objected to was wearing new shoes. Even though we always had them properly fitted and he was allowed some choice in the matter of colour, he would always refuse to walk anywhere for a few days after we purchased them. I'm sure that they didn't rub him – I think he just wanted the old ones back. Quite often, when we were in the car, he would take his shoes off and throw them at me, but there was not a lot I could do while I was driving. Once I arrived at the shops to discover that one of Pete's shoes was missing. I knew that he had been wearing both shoes when he climbed into the car and, as I always kept the windows closed, could only conclude that he'd thrown it through the open sunroof.

One of Pete's Christmas presents in 1982 was a doll's carrycot and bedding that he played with a lot and seemed to enjoy. He liked to put his 'baby' into the cot upside down and then suffocate it with the blankets – a bit of a worry, as we were hoping to present Peter with a baby brother or sister the following year.

Sadly, that was once again not to be, as I miscarried in February '83, although this time, thankfully, it was all over with very quickly and I didn't have to be apart from Pete for more than a couple of days.

On the Move Again

In May 1983 we moved to Bankfield Road in Shipley, having sold our house in Bingley to Andy's Mum and Dad. Pete seemed quite happy with this arrangement and enjoyed having Grandma and Grandad to stay with us for a few weeks prior to our move.

He liked the new house, particularly the windows, which had low sills that he could see over all by himself. He used to love watching the streetlights come on and would stand waiting, as soon as it started to grow dark, shouting 'Light on!' as soon as the first one lit up. He also coined the phrases 'black dark' and 'blue dark', to tell us if it was time for him to go to bed or not – 'blue dark' meaning that it was still too early! This was something of a nuisance in the summer, when 'black dark' didn't appear at all some nights. However, he was usually tired enough to go to bed despite the sky being the wrong colour.

Having moved to Shipley, we found ourselves having to negotiate the notorious Saltaire roundabout on a fairly regular basis, which was (and still is) the scene of some pretty terrible driving.

On one occasion, when Pete was travelling in the car with his Dad, Andy had to brake sharply when a car cut across in front of him. Before he could utter a sound, a little voice from the back shouted, 'Pillock!' I can't think where he picked up that expression but just in case you're wondering, Andy assures me that the rebuke *was* aimed at the other driver!

My sister Janet came to stay at our new home for a few days during the summer holidays with her son Jamie and, as the weather was lovely, we all went down to Saltaire so that we could go boating on the river. For some reason, Peter was having an 'off' day and was being particularly unfriendly towards Aunty Janet, which was very unusual, as he was normally very fond of her. We rowed upstream, enjoying the warm sunshine and beautiful scenery, all the time trying to distract Pete from his grumpy state by pointing out the ducks and the people walking along the riverbank.

Peter was having none of this and suddenly turned to my sister, glared at her and said, 'Janet, get out!' I'm not sure if he expected her to swim to the side or to walk on water but he was most put out by the fact that she didn't comply with this order until we were safely restored to the riverbank.

Although Peter's behaviour was proving something of a challenge, he was still generally a happy, friendly little boy. He was feeding himself quite well and would attempt to dress himself. He was using longer, more complex sentences and knew just what to say to raise a laugh. From time to time we would try to get him out of nappies at night without success, but he was using the toilet during the day, so overall we were quite pleased with his progress. He enjoyed riding on a small tricycle (although he couldn't pedal it) and would also go for short walks round the neighbourhood with one of us holding his hand.

In the late summer of '83, we were introduced to another family on the 'Give Mum a Break' scheme, who lived in Eldwick. David and Joan were keen for Pete to stay overnight with them and very kindly looked after him for us on many occasions over the next few years, giving Pete a whole new range of experiences and giving us some welcome respite. They had two children, Ian and Janet, who were a good few years older than Pete and therefore able to help with keeping him entertained.

They also had a dog, a Springer spaniel called Pepper that Pete liked to play with. He liked to throw toys for the dog to chase but managed to throw one of them right through a large double-glazed window one day, much to his astonishment and David and Joan's consternation. It is very much to their credit that they didn't stop looking after him after that episode.

Double Trouble

By the autumn of '83, I was pregnant again and had to go into hospital straight away for 'bed rest'. I was admitted at the beginning of November and wasn't allowed home until mid-January '84 (after having an amniocentesis), which meant another long separation from Pete.

Gran and Grandpa came to the rescue once again, collecting Pete from school when Andy couldn't. Pete would be brought to see me each day at the 'opsital', but was not keen to stay too long. I was in a side ward on my own but I think he would have preferred a wider audience and usually wanted whoever had brought him to take him for a walk round.

At the time, he seemed to accept the new routine fairly well but it must have been a difficult period for him. He celebrated his 4th birthday while I was in hospital, although I was allowed home for a few days over Christmas.

We had bought him a bright blue plastic pedal car for Christmas, which he adored. He would drive himself round the house or the garden and pretend that he was going to work or the shops. Andy gave him some old keys on a key ring, which also delighted him.

When I came home from the hospital in January, I was supposed to take things fairly easy – difficult with an active and increasingly stubborn 4-year-old to deal with. Things weren't too bad to begin with; I had a lot of support from the family and from Pete's 'Give Mum a Break' carers and I also employed a cleaner, which was a definite bonus.

Unfortunately, a week before the Easter holidays, Peter came home from school with an upset tummy that turned out to be dysentery. After the first few days when he was clearly unwell, he soon recovered his 'bounce' but was unable to return to school until he had been given the all-clear by the environmental health officer, which he didn't get until the day before the school broke up for the two-week spring Bank Holiday. I was absolutely exhausted by the time he went back to school!

Pete had always enjoyed looking at books and listening to stories and was very keen to learn to read. While he was off school I made some flash cards and he was soon able to read over twenty of them without any trouble. He enjoyed showing off this new skill to anyone who would listen, so was able to practise regularly.

He was pleased to return to school, having missed both his friends and the daily routine. He was also increasingly aware of my expanding tummy and would often pat or kiss it and say 'New baby – asleep'. I was hoping that he would be as gentle when the baby was born.

When Hannah, his sister, made her entrance into his life on June 23rd 1984, he accepted her very well and was very loving towards her at first, if

31

sometimes a little rough. He often wanted to pick her up and cuddle her. I soon realised that the only way to be sure she wasn't being dragged out of her carrycot by the neck was to put it inside the big cot, so that Pete couldn't reach her – not that he wanted to hurt her, he just didn't realise his own strength.

However, when the novelty of his new baby sister had worn off, Peter's behaviour took a definite turn for the worse. Although I tried to include him in as many aspects of Hannah's care as possible and to ensure I spent time with him alone, he was obviously very jealous, as many children are of a new sibling. He would take every opportunity to misbehave, particularly during feeds. Emptying cupboards was a favourite trick, as was cramming anything he could lay his hands on into the washing machine and switching it on. He enjoyed throwing his toy cars around in his bedroom, often breaking the light bulb or taking chunks out of the walls.

Thankfully, he didn't take his displeasure out on Hannah too regularly, but it seemed as though he couldn't control himself. When I rebuked him for his naughty behaviour, he would sob, making me feel like a heartless brute. But he would often repeat this behaviour again the minute my back was turned.

You Win Some – You Lose Some

The long summer holidays were always difficult to fill and, with a new baby, we didn't really feel like going away on holiday for very long. We had a couple of weekends away but didn't venture very far, as it was such an effort. Andy took a bit of time off work, which was helpful but, even so, there seemed to be a lot of time to fill.

Pete was very interested whenever our cleaning lady, Joan, came to the house. He would follow her round like a little puppy, constantly under her feet and getting in the way. She was very patient with him and let him pass her the clothes and pegs if there was any washing to hang out. He liked to hide the duster and would switch off the vacuum cleaner at the plug when she was in the middle of using it, which must have been disconcerting for poor Joan.

He did settle down again after the summer holidays and school seemed to have a calming effect on him. His sense of humour returned and he would apologise more readily for his misdeeds, although he did go through a very irritating phase of saying 'Ha-ha' when he had done or said something he knew was wrong.

But just as we thought things were improving, Pete was moved out of the nursery into the reception class at school, which unsettled him yet again. He was also given an eye-patch to wear by the ophthalmic consultant at L.G.I., which he wasn't too thrilled about, although it did lead to yet another nickname – Pirate Pete.

The speech therapist at Greenfield School suggested that I should spend some time observing Pete in the classroom and this did prove beneficial. Pete seemed reassured by my presence and his behaviour at home improved. I also started to attend his school swimming sessions, which he enjoyed. I think it helped him realise that I could spend time with him without Hannah always being there.

During this period he mastered using the toilet alone, although he preferred to sit down rather than doing a stand-up 'big boy's wee-wee' as he called it. He was rapidly becoming more independent in his personal care and wanted to bath himself and wash his own hair. He didn't want me in the bathroom with him, so I used to hover outside, just in case he got into difficulties or started to run the hot water too fast.

He could dress himself, with help on buttons, but the only way I could get him to do this in the mornings was to make him get dressed before he had his breakfast. If he wasn't ready, he had to go to school hungry. It seems cruel but otherwise he would have let me dress him without ever doing it himself.

Peter's language seemed to come on very quickly at this time and he started to use a lot more negatives, such as 'Don't wash my face', 'Don't sing that song', etc. He coined another new phrase, when he announced that he had a 'ghast' up his nose and then proceeded to show it to me. I had chastised him in the past for not keeping his nose clean and had commented that it was ghastly. Pete had obviously misunderstood and thought that this referred to the large green lump on the end of his finger.

A favourite question was "What's been doing?" whenever anyone new entered his life. He also wanted to know what people had eaten that day. That's still one of his favourite topics of conversation and he's always amazed if anyone can't actually remember.

Despite the improvement in his language he did, however, start to stutter, which we were rather concerned about until we realised that he was copying another boy from his class at school. Pete has always been a great mimic and still drives us mad by copying the speech patterns and mannerisms of many of his friends. Annoyingly, he often chooses to copy people with the most irritating habits.

One day, he was staying with Andy's youngest sister, Alison and began talking with an intonation that was clearly not his own.

"Who are you talking like, in that silly voice?" she asked.

Turning to her, with a look of complete innocence on his normally cheeky face, Pete replied, "You!"

(I had better make it clear that I am not accusing Alison of having irritating habits!)

His reading dropped off a bit when he was about five years old, partly because we were finding it hard to fit in the sessions and also due to Pete being less interested. Then one day, he suddenly wanted to do the flashcards again, so we made the effort and restarted his lessons. He soon picked it up again and could build simple sentences very well.

He was also starting to make some progress with counting and very simple sums, using numbers from 0 to 10. He liked to draw and could follow instructions to draw straight lines or circles. He would produce pictures of a washing machine, a car or Grandma and Grandad's caravan - his favourite subjects.

Pete's health was good at this time, although we were very disappointed to find that he needed two fillings when he visited the dentist for his routine check-up. Pete never minded going to the dentist and had a wall covered in stickers to show what a good boy he'd been on his visits to the surgery.

We had always taken great care with brushing Pete's teeth and had avoided giving him sweets or sugary foods. In fact, he would happily hand round a box of chocolates without ever thinking to take one for himself. It wasn't until Hannah cottoned on to what was in the box that he realised what he'd been missing!

In May '85, I decided to take Pete riding at a local stable run by a lovely lady called Beverley Kaye, who already had a couple of pupils with learning difficulties. Beverley was really good with Pete, explaining clearly what she wanted him to do and always speaking to him in a calm voice. After a few weeks, Pete really looked forward to his lessons, particularly when his friend Craig, another Greenfield School pupil, started to attend.

The pony Pete rode was called Jubilee and Pete talked about her often. When the weather turned colder, Craig was unable to attend for health reasons, so I decided that I would take his place. I had never ridden before but had confidence in Beverley's teaching. My horse was called Chipper but Pete was always adamant that I should ride Brandy, an elderly donkey that had been put out to grass at the stables.

Pete also had riding lessons at school later on but, sadly, the whole activity came to an abrupt end when he was picked up and plonked on to a horse that wouldn't stand still for him to mount. Although Pete had always enjoyed his lessons, he was understandably quite nervous of horses when he was on the ground and mounting was always something that needed to be handled carefully. Unfortunately, this episode had a lasting impression on Pete and he didn't want to go riding anymore. This was a great shame. It was one of the few activities that he and Hannah could share.

Pete also joined a gym club that was held in Greenfield School on one evening each week during term time. He behaved very badly at the club, nipping the other children and constantly trying to escape. He also attended a play scheme at school for two hours each morning during one week of the summer holiday, which gave me a bit of a break but backfired because his behaviour was once again very poor. We concluded that being in school at different times, with different people, confused him, so when the gym club restarted in the autumn we didn't bother to send him.

Challenging Behaviour

His behaviour over the summer holidays sank to an all-time low. In the house, I had to have eyes in the back of my head and couldn't relax for a moment, as he would cause damage to the house, his toys and even Hannah.

I didn't dare leave them alone together for long. Depending on what mood he was in, sometimes I wouldn't leave them at all. Although they often played beautifully together, Pete would lash out at Hannah if he was frustrated by anything, such as not being able to manipulate a toy. Sometimes, he would knock her to the floor and at least once, he held her by the hair and banged her head repeatedly on the floor.

Going out, either shopping or visiting people, was exhausting and I often had to hold him to me, with my arms and legs wrapped right round him, just to stop him from running around, grabbing at things. On one occasion in the local greengrocers, I had to pin him to the counter and get another customer to hold his hands, so that I could pay for my vegetables!

On a visit to the Alhambra theatre to see The Sooty Show, I had to practically sit on him for two hours. It seemed like he had been over-wound but he never 'ran down' until, thankfully, he collapsed into bed at night. Although he always went to bed without any bother, he would wake up as soon as daylight appeared, so in the height of summer he would be up from 4am, full of energy and raring to go. I wonder now that I didn't do him permanent damage, because there were many occasions when he goaded me beyond the limit of endurance.

I often had to give him a sharp slap on his hand or the back of his leg, just to put a stop to whatever he was doing, in a similar way to how you would deal with someone who was hysterical. The temptation to slap his face was great and I had to use all my will power not to do it. I wanted to have him fitted with a switch that I could turn to the 'Off' position when I'd had enough.

Just before the end of the summer holiday, I had made an appointment to see Professor Smithells as I felt that we needed some professional advice about Pete's behaviour. The day I'd stood in the bathroom listening to Hannah scream was truly terrible and I knew that if I didn't get help soon, I would no longer be able to cope.

Professor Smithells arranged for us to see a child psychologist. He also suggested we should let Peter have residential respite care for a couple of weeks but I couldn't bring myself to do that. Joan and David, his 'Give Mum a Break' carers, kindly offered to have Pete on a more regular basis for overnight stays, with which I felt more comfortable.

Amazingly, they also volunteered to have Hannah to stay over too, so at the age of about 14 months, off she went with her little suitcase and her 'spare earrings' (of the plastic clip-on variety) to spend her first night away from us.

The psychologist suggested various strategies to control Pete's behaviour, including a visit to a dietician to see if Pete was allergic to any foods. For the duration of two weeks, Pete (and we) had to go on a 'total exclusion' diet that cut out all the foods that caused allergies. We had wondered if any of the additives, increasingly found in processed foods, might be affecting him but after two weeks of eating only lamb, chicken, rice and rice products, a very limited range of fruit and vegetables, Soya milk and oil and kosher margarine, we had to admit that we could see no change in his behaviour. At least we had tried and, although we were all heartily sick of our very limited diet by the end of the two weeks, Pete was so glad to return to 'normal' food that his behaviour did improve slightly for a few days.

Another suggestion the psychologist made was to use a wall chart to record Pete's behaviour. The chart was sectioned off into specific periods of the day. If he went for a whole period without having to sit on the 'naughty buffet' – a high stool that Pete couldn't climb down from unaided - we would stick a two pence coin to the chart with Blu Tack. When Pete had eight coins, he could take them to the shop to buy himself a Mars Bar as a reward. (Those were the days when a Mars Bar cost only 16p.)

The psychologist continued to support us, and Pete's speech therapist also arranged for me to attend some deep relaxation sessions with her, which was a great help. Life didn't change overnight but things were improving and I felt more in control. We had definite strategies for dealing with Pete and, although it was hard sticking to them, we quickly realised that this was the only way we were going to modify his behaviour.

Rub – A – Dub - Dub

Pete was still fascinated by washing machines and tumble dryers and always wanted to look at (and preferably use) any machines that he came across when we were out visiting. Our cleaning lady, Joan, had a twin-tub machine that enthralled Pete, as it was completely different from our front-loading washer. When we visited her house he always wanted her to use it. He was also delighted to find that other people sometimes had washers or dryers in places other than their kitchens or utility rooms and liked nothing better than to discover a machine in someone's cellar, bathroom or - better still - garage.

His fascination with these machines had once nearly led to disaster. One day, when he was about six and Hannah about eighteen months old, Pete disappeared. I had been round most of the house, looking in each room and calling for him, when I realised I hadn't seen Hannah either.

I eventually found her in the utility room, standing in front of the tumble dryer with a guilty look on her face. I asked her if she'd seen Pete. Instead of replying, she just stepped to one side. There was Pete, *inside* the dryer, beaming out at me with a huge grin on his face.

"Who put him in there?" I asked Hannah, disbelief making my voice louder than it needed to be.

"He climbed in by himself."

"Who shut the door?" I demanded.

"I did."

"Whatever did you do that for?"

"Pete told me to!"

Thankfully, he never did that again and at least he hadn't asked her to switch it on!

In later years, when he was walking home alone from the bus stop after school one day, Pete passed by the home of some neighbours of ours and, seeing the door ajar, paused to look at their washer and dryer that were kept in the porch. The temptation to go in and have a look was too great for him to resist and to fiddle with them obviously even greater. I would have loved to have seen their faces when they discovered that their clean but still wet clothes in the washing machine had miraculously been transferred to the tumble dryer and were now perfectly dry!

One Step Forward, Two Steps Back

Having made such an early and promising start with his reading, we were very disappointed when Pete lost interest in books. We had established the routine of doing the flashcards with Peter after bath time, when he was reasonably calm and ready for a more sedentary activity. While Hannah played quietly with her toys, Andy or I would go through Pete's flashcards with him, until we judged that he'd had enough.

One evening, when Pete was struggling with one of the words, Hannah looked up from what she was doing and said, "Peter, it says 'minibus'".

I laughed. "O.K., Little Miss Cleverclogs, what does this one say?" and held up another card. To our surprise, she read it correctly and went on to read several more. She was only seventeen months old, but as she'd been talking fluently from the age of ten months, we probably shouldn't have been so amazed.

After that, it was hard not to let her join in with the reading sessions, as she had obviously been taking note when we had been working with Pete. The downside of this was that Pete soon realised Hannah could read more easily than he could and was less keen to practise. We gave up the joint sessions but sadly, the damage was done. Pete's reading has not progressed much further since then.

The Health Visitor that we had at that time wanted Andy and I to take Hannah along to the Association for Gifted Children, as she was clearly a very bright child. We discovered that the nearest branch was in York. Because of all our commitments with Peter, we just didn't feel that we could possibly fit in anything else, so I'm afraid that we never went along. I don't think that we significantly hindered her progress, as she eventually gained a place at Oxford, to read English, but I did feel guilty about it at the time.

During the Christmas holiday of 1985, Pete took a major leap forward by finally not wearing a nappy at night. He had gone to stay with his carers, Joan and David, and for some reason I forgot to pack a nappy. Pete stayed dry all night, so we decided to try him without a nappy at home. From then on, he almost always stayed dry, which was great for us and must have felt much better for him. On the odd occasion when he did have an 'axtinet' (accident), he would change his pyjamas and strip his own bed, without being asked.

Pyjamas came to be something of an obsession with Pete. Even now, he loves to wear unusual combinations of clothing in bed. He always likes to receive new pyjamas but has been known to go to bed wearing dressing up clothes!

In the spring we were introduced to some new carers, Geraldine and Roy, who lived in Bingley. Geraldine was a non-teaching assistant at a special school in Shipley, so we felt she would know how to cope with Pete. Roy had a large van that Pete thought was great. They also had a dog, called Halewood, of which Pete grew very fond.

In fact, we did think about moving Pete to the school where Geraldine worked, as action taken by the teachers' union at Greenfield meant that there was insufficient lunchtime cover and the children had to come home for lunch one week in every four. As the school day was only from 9.30am until 3pm with an hour for lunch, and I was still providing transport for Pete, this meant I spent all day driving backwards and forwards. Poor Hannah was in and out of the car like a fiddler's elbow!

Fortunately, Grandpa kindly stepped in and picked Pete up at lunchtime each day on the relevant weeks, so that took the pressure off. Pete enjoyed riding in Grandpa's car but the change in routine was not helpful to his overall progress. Thankfully, the L.E.A. eventually provided lunchtime supervisors so we didn't have to move Pete to another school, which would have caused even more disruption to his life.

Looking back through our personal diaries and Pete's home/school diaries from this period, I realise just how busy our lives were. We were still involved with the Down's Children's Association, Mencap and the Toy Library. I had also joined the Council for Voluntary Services and was on the Parent Teachers Association.

Apart from the regular sessions at all these organisations, there were the inevitable fund-raising events – flag days, fetes, etcetera – all of which seemed to feature pretty often. Andy became treasurer of our local branch of Mencap and was also a governor at Pete's school. Aside from all this were Pete's hospital appointments, at least one a month, plus the usual activities that all parents with children take part in, such as gym clubs, riding and swimming. Andy and I also tried to have a social life of our own and, thanks to our parents and various other people who kindly babysat, we were able to do this. The only thing I can't work out is how we ever had the energy to go anywhere!

A New Job For Dad

In April 1986 Andy started a new job in Harden, only a few miles from our home in Shipley, which meant he didn't spend so long on his daily commute. However, he did have to travel abroad on a fairly regular basis, to Paris, Barcelona and Krefeld in Germany. Even though we always had someone to stay with us while he was away, Pete was never happy about Andy's absences. Most often, Gran and Grandpa would stay (3) but other times we had Grandma and Grandad or Pete's older cousin, Andrew.

The only positive aspect of Andy going away on business, as far as Pete was concerned, was the excitement of what Dad would bring back as a present for him. He soon cottoned on to this element of Dad's travels and would usually ask what present he'd brought before Andy even had a chance to take off his jacket. His little face would light up whenever Andy brought him a car, especially if it was a replica of one we had once owned. He had a wooden ramp that Grandpa had made for him and he would send his cars speeding down it. They never lasted very long before their wheels dropped off but he certainly got a lot of pleasure out of them.

Pete was often rather heavy-handed with things, generally because of his difficulty with fine-motor control, and he could become very frustrated. If he was in a particularly bad mood we would sometimes let him have a boxing session with us, which helped to relieve his ill humour. He had a pair of fairly soft, padded boxing gloves and Andy or I would put on a pair of sheepskin mittens and let him take a swing at us. We had to go back to our 'corners' at the end of each round, pretend to have a drink and then spit it out, just like Pete had seen boxers do on television.

Pete could hit fairly hard but obviously, Andy could keep out of his reach pretty easily and absorb any punches he managed to land without too much trouble. I, on the other hand, quite often let him get too near and sometimes came off rather the worse for our encounters.

Occasionally, if Pete was in a good mood, Hannah would don a little pair of sheepskin mittens or thick socks and they would have a game of 'bunching', as Pete called it, but this was always under heavy supervision. However, Hannah soon learnt to hold her own and Pete became less keen to take on his sister at this game.

Pete's behaviour was still very mixed. With the benefit of hindsight, I now realise that his life was probably too full of activity. We were always keen that he should have the same opportunities and experiences as any other child of his age and had always been encouraged to keep him well stimulated but it may have been just too much for him to cope with. He loved routine and, generally, as long as his life ran on predictable lines, he was quite happy. When anything out of the ordinary occurred, such as Dad going away on business, it would throw him completely. Unfortunately, life doesn't often run to plan and, even now, we find that unforeseen changes tend to upset him

What Was That Again?

Despite being able to articulate his needs fairly well, Peter has always found it difficult to express his feelings and could never tell us why he had done something. If, for instance, I asked him why he had broken a light or nipped Hannah, he would reply that it was wrong or naughty but couldn't give a reason for his actions.

He also sometimes muddled words up and we would spend hours trying to work out the meaning of something that he had said. He used some comical expressions without realising they were funny. Coming into the bedroom when I was applying a roll-on deodorant, Pete stood looking at me with a puzzled expression on his face and then asked, "Why are you polishing your oxters?"

'Oxters', for those unfamiliar with the Scottish word, are armpits, and he'd picked the word up from my sister Janet who lived in Scotland at the time. Ever since then, applying deodorant has been referred to as 'polishing one's oxters' in our family.

Another favourite expression of Pete's was, 'What a lot of things', usually uttered when there were too many objects for him to count.

One day, when Andy's younger sister, Kath, came to visit, he flew across the room in delight, to be scooped into her open arms. Before she had chance to say a word, Pete pulled at the front of her low-necked tee shirt, peered down and announced to the assembled company, 'What a lot of things!'

We also found him sitting at the kitchen table one day, singing Away in a Manger to a lump of cheddar. When we asked him what he was doing, he pointed and said, 'It's Little Lord Cheeses'! His brain must work along similar lines to the spell check on the computer, as he always tries to make sense of unfamiliar words and often ends up on completely the wrong track.

Once, when we were preparing for a family party, I asked Pete to take a dish of green olives to put on a small table. He picked up the dish and then asked, "Shall I take these black Billies as well?

For a moment I couldn't think what on earth he meant but then the penny dropped. My Mum was one of five children, with an older sister called Olive and a younger brother called Billy. Pete had assumed that if the green-coloured things were known as 'Olives', then the black ones had to be 'Billies'. I'm afraid we still use that expression sometimes, which must rather confuse our guests.

Dib, Dib, Dib

When Pete reached the age of eight, we enquired at our church if he could join their Cub pack. It turned out that their Akela was just about to retire (had she realised who - or what - was coming?) and they hadn't been able to find anyone to replace her. Hannah's godfather, Allen Pollard, suggested that the Cub Scout leader at Saltaire United Reformed Church might be willing to accept Pete into her pack and we made arrangements to meet with her.

41

Barbara Lawson, Shipley 5th's Akela, kindly agreed to let Pete attend her Wednesday evening group and assigned a 'minder', an older boy called Jason, to keep an eye on him. I'm sure that poor Jason had no idea what he was letting himself in for!

Pete enjoyed going to Cubs but really hated it when they did 'The Grand Howl' at the end of each session. For the uninitiated, this is where the Cubs squat down and shout, as loudly as possible, "A-ke-la, we'll do our best!" The 'Sixer' (leader of a group of six Cubs) then shouts, "Cubs, do your best!" and they respond, "We will do our best!" When Akela realised how upset Pete was by all the shouting, she asked the Cubs to do it in a whisper, gradually increasing the volume week by week until it reached a level he could cope with.

On Wednesday, April 13th 1988, Pete was invested, receiving his neckerchief, woggle and various badges. He was really proud of himself and looked very cute in his uniform. **(Plate 4)** The Cubs and the leaders were all great with Pete, even though he was very challenging at times, sometimes nipping the other boys and throwing things at the lights in the Cub hut. He quickly learnt that the boys would carry his rucksack when they went on walks and he would let them run round after him, even though he was perfectly capable of doing most of the activities by and for himself.

Akela taught Pete to tie his shoelaces, which Pete has taken every opportunity to practice ever since. His shoes always have at least twenty knots in each lace but sadly, he can never manage to untie them, so we still spend hours un-knotting them, much to his disgust. He is quite happy to slide them on and off his bendy feet without ever undoing them, and always re-knots the laces as soon as our backs are turned. If the laces ever came out of their bows, Pete would say with great disgust, "They've come done" – another of his little sayings that has persisted over the years.

Just after he joined the Cubs, it was the annual Scout Job week ('Bob-a-Job' in our day), which Pete was very keen to join in with. We asked one or two of our neighbours if they would find some simple tasks for him to do, which he carried out very well indeed without being silly, and was gratified to receive his payment. The following Wednesday, when he arrived at Cubs, he was most disgruntled to find he had to hand over all the money to Akela, having thought that it was for him to keep!

The assistant Cub leader, Martin (or 'Bagheera' to the Cubs) invited Pete, along with the rest of the Cub pack, to join a guard of honour at his wedding. By one of those strange coincidences that happen from time to time, Martin was marrying Michelle, the girl who was (and still is) my hairdresser.

Unbeknown to us at the time, Pete charmed the driver of the wedding car into letting him sit in it. Having settled himself comfortably behind the wheel of the Rolls Royce, he found out how to switch the windscreen wipers on and off and where the switch was for the 'flashy lights' (hazard warning lights to you and me). He then locked himself in and refused to open the door. Presumably someone eventually managed to threaten or cajole him into opening it before the bride and groom came out of the church but I'll bet the chauffeur was less willing to let a small boy sit in the driving seat after that.

Digressing slightly, Pete once locked me out of the car in Leeds. He was probably only about five or six at the time and I had taken him for one of his regular check-ups at the ophthalmic clinic at Leeds General Infirmary. I left him strapped in his seat in the car while I put money in the parking meter. When I turned back to the car to get him out, I discovered to my horror that he had leaned forward and locked the driver's door. He could not be persuaded to unlock it and would probably have found that difficult. Although this was, of course, long before the days of central locking, I always kept all the other doors locked and had foolishly left the keys in the ignition.

I was on the point of hysteria when a kindly traffic warden (yes, they do exist!) came along and saw my predicament. She fished in her huge black shoulder bag and brought out a large plastic bag full of keys. Amazingly (and slightly worryingly) one of them fitted my car and we were able to get Pete out. He was completely untroubled by all the fuss and had probably enjoyed watching all that had gone on but I had learnt my lesson and never left the keys in the ignition again.

To return to my theme. Once a month, the Cubs would attend Saltaire URC for Church Parade and Pete was delighted whenever it was his turn to carry the flag, the end of which rested in a leather holster supported by a strap worn over the shoulder. Although I was always very proud of him, I was also worried that he would put out someone's eye with the flagpole, as he never really managed to control it. I still have memories of various people leaping up to catch the 6-foot-long pole as it veered from side to side, as Pete turned to grin widely at the congregation.

Before entering church, Akela would always remind the Cubs to remove their caps and, at the end of the service, to put them back on again. If she didn't say it quickly enough, however, Pete would chime in with "Caps off!" or "Caps on!" and this eventually became his regular job.

If he had behaved well at Cubs, we would allow him to call at the fish and chip shop in Saltaire on our way home. If he'd been 'really brilliant', he was allowed to go to the fish shop by himself, which always delighted him. The frontage was made of glass, so we could keep an eye on him from the car and it was delightful to watch him go marching proudly up to the counter with his money clutched in his grubby little hand. Unfortunately, one evening he marched up to the door, failed to notice it was shut and walked straight into it. It didn't put him off going again but he was always very cautious after that.

Pete moved up into the Scout group a year later than the other boys, as we were all in agreement that he needed an extra year with the Cubs, in order to mature a little more. The Scout leaders were equally patient with him and he continued to enjoy the company of the other boys, who still ran around after him. Pete was persuaded to join in with many activities that I would never have dreamed of him being able to take part in. He went canoeing, camping and hiking, including a midnight hike. I'm not sure that he was too bothered about the walk itself but he really enjoyed having a picnic in the dark and being able to shine his torch around!

'Eyes and Ears and…'

Shortly after he joined the Cubs, we discovered that despite his dislike of 'The Grand Howl', Pete was suffering from a slight hearing loss, so we added another consultant to our visiting list. Pete's teacher at that time picked up on the problem at school. I'm afraid that we had just assumed that Pete was ignoring us when he didn't respond to our commands or questions, particularly as he always seemed to be able to hear the rattle of a Mars Bar wrapper at fifty paces.

He also began wearing glasses, or should I say finding excuses *not* to wear glasses. To this day, he still won't wear them, although he has regular eye tests that always point to the fact that he should. However, I have always believed that if he put on his glasses and the world was suddenly a much clearer place, he would keep them on. As he goes to such pains to lose, hide or break his spectacles, I can only conclude that they can't make enough of a difference to him.

Pete's hearing loss, though slight, did become more noticeable as time went on, especially if he had a cold. Eventually the consultant decided that an operation to insert grommets in both Pete's ears would be necessary. An appointment was booked for him to attend the Yorkshire Clinic, where, to his delight, he discovered that his anaesthetist was 'the other Hannah's Daddy'. This was Dave Dawson, a friend and neighbour of ours who also has a daughter called Hannah. Pete was quite relaxed once he'd seen a familiar face and chatted away quite happily until Dave finally shut him up by putting him under the anaesthetic.

I waited anxiously for Pete to return from theatre but he was back very quickly, wide-awake and demanding food, having been deprived of his breakfast that morning. We knew that the operation had been a success because he kept telling everyone to stop shouting and could listen to his cassette player without deafening the rest of us.

<u>The Song and Dance Man</u>

Pete has always loved music and our holiday trips, particularly long journeys to Cornwall where we holidayed for several years, are memorable for the music we were forced to endure. Hannah and I would sit in the back of the car and play games or read, whilst Pete would claim the front seat next to Andy so that he could control the cassette player.

At first, we would have to listen to endless nursery rhyme tapes, with an occasional respite when we insisted on one of our choice. After learning 'Yellow Submarine' at school, Pete became interested in the Beatles, recognising their songs immediately if he heard them being played on the radio. He especially liked the songs of Paul McCartney (or 'Pork' McCartney, as Pete called him), so we bought him Wings albums, which he enjoyed.

On one holiday to Cornwall he kept chattering on about something that he called 'Mars Bar Face'. We pondered this for some time before we eventually connected it to My Brave Face, a track from the newly purchased Flowers in the Dirt album.

At the age of about four, Hannah wanted to learn the play the old upright piano we had inherited when we moved into Bankfield Road, so we arranged for her to have lessons with Michelle, a young piano teacher who lived nearby. One day, I heard scales being practised very nicely and went upstairs to congratulate Hannah on her good work. When I peeped round the playroom door, I was astonished to find Pete at the piano carefully picking out scales. I watched him quietly for a while and when he paused, asked him who had shown him how to play, thinking that it must have been Hannah. He replied that no one had – he'd just 'listened'. I asked if he knew anything else and he played the opening bars of the Rainbow song that they often sang at school.

When we next saw Michelle, I asked her if she would consider teaching Pete. Although she had never taught anyone with special needs, she agreed to "give him a try". That was the start of a long and very fruitful relationship, which gave Pete a lot of pleasure. He did eventually learn to read simple music and having once learnt a tune, he could always remember it.

In later years, Linda Gunn encouraged his love of music at Braithwaite School and John Froud, from Shipley Baptist church, taught him guitar. Because of his short fingers, he has always found changing chords difficult, so John usually taught him to play tunes in the classical style, which Pete mastered slowly but more easily.

Pete loved the annual church concerts at Saltaire and would watch the videos over and over again. His particular favourite was the year when Andy and Dick Clark performed their *piece de resistance* – Andy miming along to Chris de Burgh's Lady In Red and Dick wearing a red dress, blonde wig and dancing around in the background. For anyone unfamiliar with Dick, he is not a sylph-like chap and the sight of him coyly peeping from behind a lace fan brought tears of laughter to many an eye. Pete still plays the video from time to time and, whenever the church concerts are mentioned, he will always recall that particular sketch.

His other favourite sketch was 'Fred's Dead', which we first saw at Bradford Diocesan Family Camp. At Pete's insistence, this was given another airing at a church concert, with Pete playing the part of 'Fred'. Never one to miss an opportunity, he fell to his 'death' with great gusto, dissolving the audience into fits of laughter. Not content to lie quietly, though, he kept on raising his head to make sure that everyone was still watching, causing even greater hilarity.

The Great Escapes

Pete always liked to play outside and at Bankfield Road we were lucky enough to have a reasonably large garden surrounded by high walls and hedges. We had a climbing frame with a slide, a swing and enough paved areas for Pete to ride his various tricycles, pedal cars and go-karts over the years.

Worryingly, Pete was a great escape artist. Although we had very secure gates bolted from the outside, if ever he had the opportunity he would be off, usually pedalling his go-kart or the large Chopper-style tricycle (which he referred to as the 'free-wheelie' bike), that we had on loan from the Toy Library.

On more than one occasion, I had to get the car out to go looking for him. Living as we did at the crossroads, Pete had a choice of directions in which to go, although he rarely chose uphill as it was too much like hard work. I have found him at the houses of various friends and neighbours, halfway to Cottingley (trying to visit a friend from school) and across the main road at the petrol station (thankfully having used the footbridge), where he was trying to charm the assistant into letting him have a Mars Bar as he had no money with him.

One day, he disappeared from the garden when Hannah was on the potty. She was still very small and I obviously couldn't leave her but neither could she be induced to hurry. I was getting frantic about Pete and in the end had to

46

contact my next-door-neighbour. She came round to sit with Hannah while I went looking for him, by which time he was a good distance from home.

He also liked to play football and cricket in the garden, preferably with Dad but, under sufferance, with Hannah or myself when Andy wasn't available. He couldn't always make contact with the cricket ball but when he did, he could slog it quite a distance and took great delight in hitting it out of the garden. It was almost as if he were trying to make the point, that if he couldn't get out, then he'd set something else free. We had to make it a rule that if he hit the ball out of the garden three times, we stopped playing, as our poor neighbours must have been fed up with having to duck! He also used to aim the football at whoever was in goal, rather than trying to get the ball past them, which could be a pretty painful experience.

Indoors, Grandpa made wooden bars to go across Pete's bedroom window, so that he couldn't climb up onto the windowsill. A window lock prevented him from throwing things out, although if he really wanted to do it, he would just go find another window that wasn't locked. Many of the doors in the house had a bolt at the top, well beyond Pete's reach, so that he couldn't be causing mayhem in too many rooms at once. We also had child safety gates at the top and bottom of the stairs for many years, although he became very adept at climbing over them.

Generally, being alert to the possibilities was my best defence against him being somewhere he wasn't meant to be. However, with the best will in the world, it was never possible to keep track of him all the time and he was always very quick to spot his chance to escape.

Pete and the caravan

Grandma and Grandad's static caravan, on a site at Warsill, near Brimham Rocks, provided us with many happy weekends for several summer seasons. We would set off on a Friday evening, arriving at about half past six in the evening and Andy would take the children off to the wonderful adventure playground in the woods, leaving me to unpack our belongings.

After a few false starts, we realised that it was easier to let Pete and Hannah sleep in the double bed in the separate bedroom. Andy and I made up a bed in the living room, leaving us access to the other facilities in the caravan. Usually the children were so tired after running around in the fresh air that they soon went off to sleep and didn't wake too early in the mornings.

Pete also regularly accompanied Andy on walks. They completed the Nidderdale Way, in sections of between five and eight miles, over a few weekends one summer. Pete is actually quite a good walker but, like his mother, isn't keen on steep hills and will moan and groan quite a lot if he feels there are too many.

Several of our friends had touring caravans and would regularly book on to our site, providing Peter and Hannah with lots of other children to play with. The Needham family were often around, with their three sons and baby daughter. Fascinated as he was by all babies, Pete would always latch on to Sarah who, probably because she was used to being handled by three older brothers, never objected to him picking her up – not even when he sang Miss Polly to her, using her as the dolly, which would have been fine except that he held her upside down!

Other friends who came to stay at Warsill included Pete's friend Craig with his Mum and Dad. Pete loved having his own special friend there and was always very excited when he knew that they would be around.

A major attraction for Pete, on our weekends at the caravan, was the opportunity to go out for a pub lunch, another activity that he has continued to enjoy. Pete has probably eaten more pub lunches than most other people his age and is a familiar figure in many hostelries in various parts of Yorkshire.

The Water Baby

When Pete's cousin Andrew was old enough, he registered with the 'Give Mum a Break' scheme and would sometimes take Pete to the local swimming baths, which Pete loved. After a few sessions that passed without mishap, Pete wanted Hannah to go along, too. Andrew's younger sister Suzy, a keen swimmer and diver, said that she would be happy to accompany them and keep an eye on Hannah so, after some debate, we decided to let them go. My sister Val and I dropped them all off at the swimming pool and then she and I went shopping.

We weren't away for very long but, on our return, couldn't see any of the children in the pool. Having found no sign of them in the changing rooms, we asked a member of staff if they had been seen anywhere. As Pete was fairly easy to recognise, she had no difficulty in remembering him and told us that they were all in the first aid room. We dashed in there to find Pete with blood streaming from a large gash on his chin and poor Andrew looking very worried.

When we finally got to the bottom of the story, it turned out that Pete had been trying to make Andrew jump in and had pushed him. Andrew had landed in the water without mishap but Pete had lost his balance and fallen in, catching his chin on the side of the pool on the way down.

After a visit to our G.P. and then to the nurse in the A & E department at Bradford Royal Infirmary, I thought Pete might not want to swim again. Thankfully, this misadventure didn't leave a lasting mental scar, although he still has the physical scar on his chin, now hidden under his beard. I was rather anxious for a while afterwards but it seemed that Pete had learnt his lesson, as he never again tried to push anyone into the water.

He liked to watch his cousin Suzy dive and we would sometimes go along when she took part in competitions at Shipley swimming pool. I could hardly bring myself to look as she perched on the end of the highest diving board and threw herself off in some complicated manoeuvre. Pete thought it was great and clapped his hands excitedly. I was rather worried when he announced that he would like to try it but thankfully, I think that the ladders leading to the diving boards put him off.

Over the years we spent a lot of time at the swimming baths, quite often watching Hannah's lessons. It was always difficult to know what to do with Pete while I was helping Hannah change and dry her hair, which was very long and difficult for her to deal with herself. As he grew older, it became inappropriate for him to be in the girls' changing rooms.

In the end, heart in mouth, I let him go to the café, which was upstairs above the pool, to buy himself a meal. I spoke to the staff in the café first, who were familiar with Pete, and told them to send for me if he caused any trouble. After a few practice sessions I let him go up alone, clutching just enough money in his hand to buy a small meal and a drink.

I would then help Hannah dry herself, dress and get as much moisture out of her hair as possible, all in the space of about ten minutes. By the time we joined Pete in the café, he would be halfway through his meal. It was all a bit nerve-wracking but generally, it worked reasonably well.

Crime and Punishment

Provision was eventually made for Pete to go to school by taxi, provided by the Local Education Authority. This meant that he had to be ready in good time as the taxi was sometimes early and the driver obviously didn't want to wait. As I've said before, he would occasionally be very stubborn in the mornings and refuse to dress himself. I thought I'd more or less sorted this out by not letting him have breakfast until he was dressed but one morning even this threat didn't get him moving. I tried everything I could think of – pleading, cajoling, threatening – but nothing had any effect on this stubborn little boy. In the end I sent him off in the taxi wearing his pyjamas and a pair of wellies!

49

He was occasionally very badly behaved in the taxi, kicking Iris, the long-suffering, good-natured escort, or nipping other children. We supplied a story or nursery rhyme tape for them to listen to on the journey, which helped to distract Pete but must have been mind-numbing for the taxi driver and Iris.

The taxi company generally sent one of a small team of drivers but on the odd occasion when someone was ill or on holiday, a different driver would turn up. Peter enjoyed this, as it meant there was a new car for him to ride in, and he would usually watch out of his bedroom window each morning in the hope that it would be a change from the usual taxi.

Even though he mostly enjoyed school, like most children there were some mornings he just didn't want to go. He would come up with a variety of excuses, including 'I'm too poorly' and 'It's not Monday' (which stood for any weekday.) Sometimes he didn't like the clothes I had put out for him and would hide any article of clothing that particularly offended his dress-sense that day.

He was still very keen on throwing things, particularly at light fittings, sometimes causing damage but more often just hitting the light bulb hard enough to break the filament without actually smashing the bulb. One particularly memorable day, he had five broken light bulbs to his 'credit'. He was a really good shot and rarely missed when he aimed at something – proved by the number of goldfish we ended up with after visits to the fair!

We often found cushions or socks wedged in or draped over the ceiling lights, although he would usually deny vehemently that he had thrown them. Funnily enough, though, if he had broken anything by accident, he would always own up and apologise immediately. He was also completely amazed if Hannah was ever naughty (thankfully a rare occurrence) and would sit very quietly, waiting for me to stop telling her off. If she cried he would fetch a tissue and help to dry her tears, generally behaving as though he'd never done a naughty deed in his life.

Pete also went through a phase of drinking dirty washing-up water. I have no idea why he should have done this, except of course that it obviously provoked a negative reaction the first time he did it. Deciding that we needed to put a stop to this fairly swiftly, every time he'd had a drink from the washing-up bowl we used to give him a glass of water laced with just enough salt to be unpleasant and he soon got the message that 'dirty' water wasn't very nice.

Although he made us laugh a lot, Pete was still being very challenging. The throwing was becoming a more serious problem, as he had started to throw stones in the school playground. As the staff parked their cars around the edges of the playground, Pete was sent inside at playtime on an increasingly regular basis. Shortly before his ninth birthday, this problem was threatening to spiral out of control and, in desperation, I threatened him that he wouldn't *have* a birthday at all if he continued to behave like this. He obviously didn't believe me and carried on throwing stones at the cars every time he was allowed outside.

Eventually, after discussions with the school staff, I decided to carry out my threat. On 8th December I sent him to school without mentioning his birthday at all. I had intended to go into Greenfield to join in the celebrations and apparently he kept asking where I was. He also kept reminding the staff that it was his birthday but they also ignored him. His party was cancelled and he received none of his cards or presents. I don't know who was most upset - Pete, the staff or me.

It was a terribly hard thing to do but his behaviour improved immediately. He behaved well enough all that day and the next for him to have a belated birthday party the day after at school and a small, quiet celebration with a few friends at the weekend.

In the New Year, Pete was given the job of milk monitor at school, which involved him carrying crates of milk around to each classroom. He loved doing this and for the most part did it sensibly. It was also a useful carrot that could be dangled, so if he misbehaved, he wasn't allowed to be milk monitor.

Pete did enjoy socialising (and still does) and was usually at his best when we ate out. We often received compliments from the staff in restaurants about Peter's behaviour, as he always stayed seated at the table during the meal and was polite, quite often raising a smile by calling 'Danke shoen', when his food appeared.

One of his favourite treats was to go to the Fountain pub in Heaton for fish and chips. We often went on Saturday lunchtimes and Pete became a favourite with the landlady, Joan, her husband Frank and several of the staff. He was even on first name terms with some of the regulars and loved to chat with them all.

There was an advert for Boddington's beer on the T.V. around this time, which Pete found amusing, and he liked to raise a laugh by re-enacting it. In the advert a smartly-dressed woman wiped some of the froth from a pint of beer on her face, after which a man entered the room, looking rather like James Bond: tall, dark and well dressed. However, when he opened his mouth, he spoke with a broad North Country dialect. So Pete would walk into the bar of the pub, make eye-contact with someone he knew, sniff loudly, then announce, "By 'eck, yer smell gorgeous tonight, petal!"

Peter was always well behaved, if somewhat lively, at the Fountain and a trip there was something we could use as a reward for good behaviour. However, this approach didn't always work, so Pete had to be punished for

51

behaving badly. It was always difficult to find punishments that worked, as he really didn't mind being deprived of his toys, even his go-kart or the tricycle.

In the end, we found that what really worked was to deprive him of his meals. He never starved, obviously, but when we sat down to a family dinner, Pete would get a plate of bread and butter and a glass of water. It did seem harsh but, in the end, it was the only way to make him realise that we were very cross with him.

Sometimes we would use a system of 'fines' (he was once fined two sausages for dismantling Hannah's bedside lamp) but he was never one to miss an opportunity and became very clever at locating items of food. Having taken him with me to collect Hannah from a party one day, he managed to pinch a half-eaten sausage from someone's plate, making me feel very guilty and no doubt making the other parents think that we never fed him.

Unfortunately, when he had the urge to throw something, it was as if he really couldn't stop himself and he would just have to do it, even though he knew he would be in trouble.

I sometimes used to 'set up' a punishment for him, when I knew that he was in a silly frame of mind. I did this in league with my Mum, by telling Pete that Gran had invited him for tea at her house. We would go along with this charade until Pete eventually threw something at a light or did something horrible to Hannah. Then I would ring Gran and tell her that Peter wouldn't be able to visit her after all.

He was always very remorseful when this happened and his behaviour would usually improve for a few days. Obviously, sometimes we had to stop him going to Gran's when it was a genuine visit and that was as big a hardship to us as it was to Pete. He was usually going because we needed a break and my parents would be babysitting.

We found it difficult to dissuade him from throwing objects at the ceiling light in his bedroom, so in desperation we removed the whole fitting and used a bedside lamp, which we took out every night after he'd gone to bed. It seemed drastic but we were fed up with having to replace light bulbs and, occasionally, the shade.

Somewhat to our surprise, though, Pete was very good about the washbasin in his bedroom. When we moved into the house, there was an old basin fitted in the corner and we decided to replace it with a vanity unit. From the start, Pete accepted that it was there for him to use for washing and cleaning his teeth and never did anything silly with it – except once.

When he had finally outgrown the blue car, we had borrowed another one from the Toy Library. It was bright orange and Pete loved to sit in it and drive it around. He was thrilled to bits with it and liked to keep it in his room, although it really was too big. One day, he proudly came to tell me that his new car was clean, like Daddy's. Why I didn't realise what he had done more quickly, I don't know, but when I later went upstairs, I was aghast to find that he had washed the car in the middle of his bedroom floor. The carpet was soaked and there were soapsuds everywhere. Still, at least it was nice and shiny when we returned it to the Toy Library that weekend.

He quite liked to 'pretend' play, although he had a limited repertoire of scenarios. One favourite was to use the snooker table as a bunk bed, with Pete lying underneath (thank goodness) and all his soft toys on top. He would lie under there for quite lengthy periods, so it was always a game to be encouraged. He had a huge stuffed clown (named Peter Clown if I remember rightly) that he would talk to endlessly, telling it about his day. This story usually featured the clown as the naughty individual who had done all the silly things, with Pete himself as the good boy who never put a foot wrong.

Pete had always found it difficult to verbalise exactly what made him upset, so it seemed like a major step forward when he actually said, "I don't want Dad to go to Germany." Even though we knew that Andy's travelling was triggering some of his difficult behaviour, it was almost a relief to us that Pete could recognise that it bothered him. However, as Andy had no choice about travelling abroad on a fairly regular basis, there wasn't a lot we could do other than try to explain, as simply as we could, why Dad kept disappearing. I suppose that Pete was still suffering from the insecurities of his early days, when Andy had been in Sharjah and I was in hospital.

Keys

Keys have always attracted Pete's attention, particularly car keys. He has always liked to be 'in charge' of them. These days it's not a problem, as he can remember where he's put them much better than I can but when he was younger, that wasn't always the case. Hiding the keys or dropping the latch on the door when we were outside in the garden (with the keys still in the house) were favourite tricks.

We kept a spare set at Gran's, so Grandpa would usually come to the rescue, although occasionally we would have to phone Andy at work to get his keys. Unfortunately, this was always looked upon as a treat by Peter, as Dad was sometimes too busy to come and would ask one of the company drivers to come over with the keys, giving Pete the opportunity to look at yet another 'different' car or even, one lucky day, a motorbike.

We often looked after the house of our friend and neighbour, Sue Pedley, when she went on holiday, and would call in to water her plants once or twice while she was away. Unlike us, Sue had a burglar alarm and I was always slightly anxious about opening her front door, then the inner porch door, before the alarm went off. For some reason I could never remember which key fitted which lock. Pete, of course, had no such problem.

One day, helping himself to her keys (which I had stupidly left within his reach), he went to her house and let himself in. What he hadn't bargained for, though, was the alarm, which nearly frightened him to death, ensuring that he didn't do that again in a hurry!

When Andy first bought a car with central locking, Pete literally thought that it was 'magic'. If he managed to get hold of the keys, he would rush to the gate at the back of the garden, lean over and lock and unlock the car until we, or one of our neighbours, spotted him. Realising that this activity was too visible, he discovered that he could operate the central locking from our bathroom window.

Our neighbours John and Cathy 'Cross-the-Road', as Pete called them, often saw his arm protruding from the window as he frantically pressed the button on the key fob. The garage door didn't need to be open for Pete to activate the central locking and he could watch the lights flashing on and off through the garage windows. It's a wonder that the batteries ever lasted more than a week!

999

Pete's fascination with vehicles didn't stop at cars. Over the years he's managed to sit in the cab of several fire engines. When the Fire Service paid a visit to the Cub group, he was the only boy allowed to sound the siren and turn on the windscreen wipers. He was also given permission to sound the horn in the police car that came to our house after Andy had earlier had his car radio/cassette stolen. If the neighbours hadn't already been aware that the police were visiting us, they certainly were once Pete had blared the horn.

At school, Pete had been having lessons in how to call the emergency services. This was of course a good idea in one respect but a bit of a problem in another, as he phoned them on a regular basis. At that time, we had one telephone in the hallway and another in our bedroom and he quickly learned that, although I could hear him if he used the one in the hall, I was less likely to catch him if he went upstairs. I have lost count of the number of grovelling apologies I have had to make to irate emergency service telephonists.

TV Times

Pete had never really shown much interest in watching television and I have to say that we had never particularly encouraged him to watch, feeling that it was not very stimulating for him. He had never shown any interest in cartoons nor wanted to watch any of Hannah's Disney films, the action being too fast for him to keep up with. He did quite like to watch videos of Postman Pat, Thomas the Tank Engine and Fireman Sam. He would watch the same video ad nauseum if we let him and, even more annoyingly, would rewind bits over and over again.

He would occasionally watch snooker or boxing on T.V., probably because the action was slow enough for him to follow. He took enough interest in the snooker for us to buy him a quarter-size snooker table, which we just about had room for in the playroom, although some of the shots had to be played from slightly strange angles.

Apart from the odd occasion when he would poke the light fitting with his snooker cue, he behaved really well and soon learnt the rudiments of the game. We brought the table with us when we moved to Hellifield in 2005 but as it was getting a bit threadbare and rather wobbly, Pete recently bought himself a new one, so he can still enjoy a game when he comes to visit us.

He doesn't understand the scoring and only considers someone to have won when the black ball is finally potted. He is quite good at potting the balls and knows in which order they have to go down and he is also adept at snookering the opposition, albeit unwittingly. We do keep score but we don't put any points on for any of Pete's foul shots, which balances the game up a bit. When it gets to the last few balls on the table, he will use 'dirty tactics', such as singing something silly or standing directly behind the pocket his opponent is aiming for. He has rather lost interest in watching snooker on T.V. now but for a time, it helped to pass an odd half hour in a quiet and calm manner.

He discovered Mr. Bean, which we were quite pleased about, as we didn't mind watching the videos with him sometimes. Again, the 'action' was very measured and the lack of speech made them easier for Pete to follow. Although the stories were quite silly, we felt that they were harmless enough. Oh! How wrong could we be!

One day, when I suddenly realised that the house was too quiet, I went upstairs to look for Pete, only to find him in our bedroom, stark naked, sitting in a cardboard box, with our small portable television lifted down from its home on our wardrobe shelf balanced precariously on a stool in front of him.

"What on earth are you doing?" I exclaimed, mystified.

"I'm Mr. Bean," Pete calmly replied.

It took me a moment to remember that yes, indeed, there was a video where Mr. Bean buys a new T.V., which he can only get to work by taking off all his clothes, sitting in the box that the television had come in and holding the aerial at a funny angle. Pete had remembered the whole episode and decided to re-enact it.

He also, more embarrassingly, acted out another Mr. Bean sketch when we were on holiday. We had taken the children to the hotel's indoor pool and Pete had jumped in, removed his swimming trunks and then swum up and down, pretending to look for them. By the time we spotted what he was doing, several other people had also noticed. We had him back into his trunks and out of the pool before he could blink and, thankfully, he never (to my knowledge) repeated that one. I think that, in the sketch, Mr. Bean lost his trunks when he dived in and Pete had obviously thought this a huge joke.

Fun and Games

Eventually, we lost our long-term carers, Joan and David, who had given up for family reasons. We did gain several new ones, which meant that we had more people to call on when we needed extra help. A couple from Shipley had volunteered to care for Pete on the 'Give Mum a Break' scheme and Pat White, a teacher from Pete's school, had also registered with them. Pete loved going to Mrs. White's house but was less sure about the others, as they had three boys who were still quite young and I think he felt that there was too much competition. He was, however, intrigued by the fact that they shared a car with another family and was always keen to find out whether it was their 'turn' to use it whenever he went to visit them.

Pete loved spending time with his older cousins and was delighted when we established a regular weekly visit to their house for tea. I would collect him from school, drive down the road just in time to meet Suzy coming out of her school gates and then drive round to the school where Aunty Val worked as a nursery nurse.

Andrew would usually arrive home on his bicycle as we pulled up outside their house and Pete and Hannah would dash off inside to be entertained by their cousins. In the summer, they would often play in the garden, while Val and I chatted and prepared the meal. Sometimes, in the winter, they would be lucky enough to be able to go sledging down Wrose Hill with Andrew and Suzy, coming back to the house freezing cold and soaking wet. **(Plate 5)**

Aunty Val would sometimes let Pete have a bath in their Jacuzzi, which he loved. She would pour a few drops of bubble bath into the water, give Pete all the bath toys and soaps-on-ropes and then leave him to disappear among the bubbles. It kept him occupied for a while, although one of us would have to keep an ear open for sounds of him getting out, as he would sometimes appear downstairs stark naked, with only the bubbles to hide his modesty, leaving a trail of wet footprints behind him.

He liked dressing up and attended several fancy dress parties as a pirate, a clown and Postman Pat, **(Plate 6)** to name but a few. One day he made us all laugh by coming downstairs dressed in a costume that Andy had hired for a fancy dress party, when Andy had dressed as Daddy Bear and I'd gone as Goldilocks. Bearing in mind that Andy is about six feet tall and Pete only about four foot three at the time, you can imagine what he looked like, the legs of the costume like Norah Batty's stockings in myriad folds around his ankles. How he managed to get himself into it (and down the stairs without tripping up and breaking his neck) I shall never know.

Indoors, Pete enjoyed playing with his cars and the garage that Grandpa had made him for a Christmas present in 1984. It was a two-storey affair with ramps, double doors at the back and an up-and-over door at the front. Gran had marked out car parking spaces on it and Pete would spend hours driving his toy cars up the ramps and parking them neatly.

Changes ahead

Pete entered his final year at Greenfield School in September 1990. His class teacher was Mrs. Whiteley, who had moved into our neighbourhood during the summer holidays and then made the mistake of taking Pete to her house after an outing in the school minibus.

As soon as Pete realised that Mrs. Whiteley was now a neighbour, he was determined she should call round for a coffee. I agreed that he should issue an invitation, which she graciously accepted. However, when I pointed out to her that Pete had mentioned that he would now be able to visit her 'every day' and that he had wanted to take some friends of ours to see her new house, her response was "I'm moving!" He did occasionally disappear down the road to see her but we managed to dissuade him from doing it too often.

As he was in his last year at Greenfield, we had to start looking round for a new school for him and the choice, as always the case in Special Education, was limited.

Our first visit was to Hayfield School in Bradford, a school to which many of Peter's friends would be going. Because we lived in Shipley, this wasn't actually on our recommended list and, if we had wanted Peter to go there, I would once again have had to provide transport. As I had just started on a floristry course at Shipley College and Hannah was now attending Saltaire First School, this was not really going to be a serious option. We felt that we had to look at the available schools in the area, in order to be able to make some sort of comparison. The school Pete was most likely to attend, for which the local education authority would provide transport, was Braithwaite School, in Keighley; a visit had been scheduled for the following spring.

In November, Peter's friend Craig moved to Biddulph, Staffordshire, with his parents. I'm not sure that Pete understood the implications of Craig's going away – that he wouldn't be moving with him to the next school - but he enjoyed the leaving party that the staff arranged at Greenfield. We kept in touch with the family and Pete and Craig have seen each other periodically over the years, attending each other's eighteenth birthday parties and visiting each other's homes from time to time.

They are always pleased to see each other but actually have little in common – Craig likes to read and watch T.V. and knows all that is happening in the soaps. He also enjoys drawing and various crafts. Pete, on the other hand, would rather be out on his go-kart or listening to his music.

After the Christmas holidays, Andy and I were invited to go to visit Brunswick Road, a respite care unit in Idle. We were not totally convinced by this idea but felt that we should go to see what they had to offer. We had been conscious that we were relying very heavily on both sets of grandparents and, although we still used the 'Give Mum A Break' scheme, it was not always possible for someone to have Pete if we wanted to go away for a whole weekend. Several people we knew from Pete's school used Brunswick for respite, so we reluctantly decided to look.

The unit had been built about five years earlier as a children's home but then changed to cater for children with special needs. They took about fifteen children at a time and provided respite care for around sixty families. At that time, most families were offered one overnight stay each week and one weekend stay per month.

Our initial visit went well. The rooms were sparse but clean and the communal areas were pleasantly decorated and comfortably furnished. The staff were friendly and the children seemed happily engrossed in a variety of activities, not just glued to the television as I had feared. Peter could visit at teatimes before trying an overnight stay. We were quickly reassured that, however challenging his behaviour might be, there could be nothing they hadn't dealt with before. All in all, we were very encouraged.

On the journey home, Andy spoke very positively about Brunswick Road and how we would benefit from Pete going there. If he noticed that I was unusually quiet, he didn't comment. We arrived home and related the details of the visit to my Mum and Dad, who had been babysitting. After they had gone home, I burst into tears.

Andy was puzzled and asked what was wrong, remarking that the place was much nicer than we dared hope. "I know," I sobbed, "and now I can't think of any reason why he shouldn't go!"

It seems barmy now but I think I had gone to Brunswick Road almost hoping that it would fail to meet our requirements, so that I would have good reason for not sending Pete there. Difficult as life was at times, I still couldn't accept that we were finding it hard to cope. I felt that letting him go to a respite care home, rather than using the 'Give Mum A Break' service, was tantamount to admitting defeat.

Reluctantly, I agreed with Andy that Pete should go for tea to see how he fared. Once again we rehearsed the reasons for doing it. We needed a break, to give ourselves some time to recharge our batteries. Hannah also needed some time alone with us, without having to play second fiddle to her brother.

We also had to accept that both sets of grandparents couldn't be expected to fill the breach. Apart from the fact that Pete could be very hard work, they also had other grandchildren and we were both very conscious of taking up too large a slice of their time.

We had to wait a little while before Pete could be slotted into the schedule but, gradually, he started to visit for tea and then occasionally stayed overnight. It was April before he was offered a regular slot, which meant we were then able to forward plan for about three months at a time. Because Pete's night at Brunswick was on a Thursday, it meant that when he had his monthly weekend stay he would be away from Thursday until Monday. This gave us the opportunity for a long weekend, especially when it fell in term-time, as he was away from first thing on Thursday morning until Monday after school.

Although initially reluctant to let him go, eventually I had to admit it had been the right thing to do. Being able to plan a weekend away without the guilt of imposing on our families was wonderful. Having one night a week when we could totally relax at home was good too. If we wanted to go out, we were lucky to have no problem obtaining babysitters for Hannah – there was always an endless supply of local teenage girls who would come and sit with her. When we went away for a weekend, we could always find someone who would look after her. I never felt guilty about abandoning her, as she always came home absolutely full of where she'd been, who she'd seen, what she'd done and, like her brother, what she had eaten.

Although there were occasional incidents at Brunswick Road (and probably more than we were ever told about), Pete seemed happy enough to go there and the staff lived up to their promise of coping with whatever he threw at them - sometimes literally. He still threw objects at light fittings and would switch the lights on and off very rapidly whenever he entered or left a room, which was exceedingly annoying. However, life was improving for us all because of the regular respite.

We still used 'Give Mum a Break' for babysitting purposes and there were several youngsters who came fairly regularly to sit with Pete while Andy and I attended MENCAP, PTA, governors' meetings etc, but it was definitely easier all round with Pete getting the bulk of his respite care at Brunswick.

59

In early February Pete had to go into the Yorkshire clinic for the insertion of new grommets. He was slightly disappointed to find that his anaesthetist wasn't Dave Dawson. Whoever it was, I think Pete must have been given a larger dose of anaesthetic, as he slept for ages after we arrived home. I was almost tempted to ask for a bottle of whatever they had used to knock him out, as the peace and quiet was lovely!

Shortly after this, I had to go into hospital for a couple of days, to have a benign lump removed from under my arm. Pete told everyone that I was going to have my 'oxters mended', which no doubt caused a lot of puzzlement. He made me a Get Well card and some biscuits at school, which he insisted on giving to me the night before I went in to hospital, rather than waiting until he came to visit the next day.

He stayed with Gran and Grandpa for one night while I was at the Yorkshire Clinic and nearly succeeded in putting them all in hospital by turning on their gas fire without igniting it. Fortunately, Gran spotted what he had done before disaster struck and had the presence of mind not to make a big fuss about it - which would have been the best way of making sure he tried to do it on every subsequent visit.

Pete was very kind to me when I returned from hospital, making me breakfast in bed unasked and sensibly putting on several loads of washing. He wasn't naughty or silly at all while he could see I was genuinely in discomfort and unable to chase round after him. As soon as I was back on my feet, however, he was back to his usual tricks.

We had noticed this aspect of his behaviour before, if one of us was unwell. He would always be gentle and caring, sitting on the edge of the bed, watching over whoever was ill while they slept. Unfortunately, in an uncanny way, he always knew the moment the crisis was over and immediately reverted to his normal, lively, cheeky self.

A big advantage of Pete getting a place at Brunswick was that I could attend my floristry course at Shipley College with a clear conscience. The manager at Brunswick had kindly offered to let Pete go for tea there on the day I attended college, so that I didn't have to come out of class early to meet him.

When I first began the course, I had arranged for the school taxi to drop Pete at Shipley College but this was never really going to work and looking back, I can't begin to imagine why I ever thought it would.

Pete officially finished school at three o'clock but as it took quite a while for the staff to help the children to put on their outdoor shoes, coats and, during the cold weather, hats, scarves and gloves as well, they would start getting the children ready shortly after two-thirty. Quite often, the taxis would arrive early and the children would be allowed to go, as the taxi drivers would have other children to collect from mainstream schools and were always keen to make a quick getaway.

This meant that Pete arrived at the college just a few minutes after three o'clock. As I didn't actually finish until three-thirty, the problem of what to do with him was a thorny one. For a couple of weeks I tried sitting him in the cafeteria, which was just outside my classroom. I bought him a drink and a bun or some crisps and told him to sit quietly until I had finished.

It was bad enough having to sneak out of the class during a lecture but when I returned I found that I had both ears tuned to possible 'noises off', rather than to whatever the lecturer might be saying.

Pete behaved reasonably well the first week, as this arrangement was a bit of a novelty. Typically, on the second occasion, having become more familiar with his surroundings, he was more confident about striking out and doing his own thing. Once again, I had my ears stretched to pick up any sounds of misdoings and when I heard the sound of tables being very noisily folded up, I knew Pete was at work.

I hastily left the classroom, to find that he was indeed busily putting all the tables away, despite the fact that he had no idea whether or not this needed doing. I think that he intended to be helpful, as he sometimes had to put away the dinner tables after lunch at school.

After that, I realised having him delivered to College wasn't a good idea, so for a while he went to my Mum and Dad's and I collected him from there. However, I wasn't really happy with that, as they already did so much for us with regard to looking after Pete. Being able to send him to Brunswick took a huge weight off my mind and Pete seemed happy enough to go.

On Friday, April 19th, we took Pete to Braithwaite School so that he could meet the staff and his fellow pupils. He already knew some of the older children who had previously been at Greenfield and there were some old friends from both the Opportunities Play Group and the Down's Children's Association.

While we were there, Pete was asked to feed the school goldfish and, best of all, was allowed to put some dirty laundry into the automatic washing machine. After the visit, we went along the road for lunch at The Turkey pub in the tiny village of Goose Eye, which Pete was to come to know well when Aunty Alison moved into an apartment there. Having had such a good day out, we were hopeful this would stick in Pete's memory as an enjoyable experience and that the change of school would not prove too traumatic for him.

As the time drew nearer for Pete to leave Greenfield School and make the move to Braithwaite, I was probably a lot more worried than he was. Although I knew that we had all done our best to prepare him for the change,

I was very aware of how difficult the upheaval would be for him and that he didn't really understand that the move was final.

Apart from that, I was sad at leaving behind so many good friends, both parents and staff. I knew that there would not be the opportunity at the new school for the same sort of support system that had sustained many of us through some dark and difficult times. We had shared our hopes and fears and I was able to cry but also to laugh with people who truly understood the problems, worries and very particular joys of raising a handicapped child.

Part Three

The boy with 'Dancing Drums'

Braithwaite School

The move to Braithwaite was pretty much as I had feared. Pete's behaviour took a definite turn for the worse as he struggled to cope with a new environment, lots of fresh faces and a completely different set of expectations.

At Greenfield, mostly, one or two teachers per year group taught the children. At Braithwaite, Pete had to get used to a different teacher for each subject, in different classrooms and to finding his way around the building.

Although the movement around school was supervised to some extent, it nevertheless presented Pete with opportunities for mischief, which he frequently took. He liked to go into the hall and move the gym equipment about or rearrange the tables and benches. He was usually caught red-handed but this didn't deter him. His home-school diaries were filled with remarks about his behaviour, which were seldom good.

We were, nevertheless, not displeased with the way that most of the staff were coping with Peter. As the teachers got to know him and grew used to his peculiar sense of fun, he gradually settled down and we were astounded at the amount of work he produced. The ones who drew out his better side were those who could share a joke with him, at the same time keeping a lid on his exuberance.

He interacted well with the games teacher, a very enthusiastic chap, who to our amazement encouraged Pete to join the Running Club, which met at lunchtimes. The children were encouraged to run round the school perimeter, at their own pace, as many times as they could manage in a session. After a certain number of laps, the children were presented with a certificate in assembly and were much praised for their efforts. Although Pete always had loads of energy, he had never been very keen on running (a bit like his mother, I'm afraid) so we were astonished that he would willingly take part in this activity.

Another of his favourites was the art teacher, a lovely lady who had a wealth of talent and patience. Pete's poor fine motor control had always hindered his being able to draw, paint and use scissors, but she always thought up projects to enable him to produce a piece of work he was happy with and could be justifiably proud of.

He was also happy in the Home Economics room, especially if he was allowed to use the washing machine. The H.E. teacher soon realised this was a very good carrot to dangle to keep Pete on task until the end of the lesson, when he was able to wash the dirty tea towels, aprons and dishcloths. He also liked cooking (and subsequent eating) but was less enthusiastic when it came to writing about what he had done.

After Pete had been at Braithwaite for about a year, Trish Pearson, who had taught him at Greenfield, joined the staff at Braithwaite as Deputy Head, much to Pete's delight. He had always liked Trish and was very pleased to see her again, particularly enjoying the aerobics sessions or discos that she organised during lunchtimes throughout the winter or in wet weather. In fact, he was so enamoured of the aerobics sessions that he used to re-enact them at home, even managing to persuade both sets of Grandparents to join in on one hilarious occasion. Sadly, I didn't have the camera to hand that day, as that would have been a good one for the archives!

He was very fond of several of the non-teaching assistants, particularly one lady whose husband had a Jowett-Javelin car. Pete was lucky enough to have a ride in it one day and he still remembers this if ever we see a similar car.

I think, though, that Pete's favourite teacher was Linda Gunn, his wonderfully talented music and drama teacher. She really brought out the best in Pete and his musical ability and love of entertaining were always put to good use in the concerts she directed.

No child was ever left out of these concerts and even those with very severe disabilities would be on stage, in costume, with some part to play. Pete, of course, was often to the fore in these productions. Gran and Grandpa usually came with me, Grandma and Grandad sometimes joined us, Andy would attend if at all possible and if Hannah was not at school, she would be there, too. Space in the hall was limited, as the parents and families of almost every child wanted to attend, as well as retired staff members, dinner ladies – you name them, they were there!

The concerts usually took place twice a year, one at Christmas and one at the end of the summer term. The Christmas one was usually a fairly typical 'Carols and Nativity' - always beautifully done and very moving.

The summer concert was always the best. Each year had a different theme that was usually linked to topics taught throughout the year and always involved drama, music and dance. The dedication shown by the staff in preparing these extravaganzas was fantastic and the results were wonderful. Pete still has the videos and cassette tapes of many of them that were sold to the enthusiastic audience after each performance and watched and listened until they were all but worn out.

I can remember hiding behind my camera, to try to disguise the fact that I had tears pouring down my cheeks, listening to a lovely teenage girl singing the Gloria Estefan song, 'Reach' which I think had been written for the Olympics that year and included the lines:

' If I could reach, higher
Just for one moment touch the sky

For that one moment in my life
I'm gonna be stronger
Know that I'd tried my very best
I'd put my spirit to the test
If I could reach.'

Hannah reminded me of another concert, when the children sang 'We are the Champions', which reduced most of the audience to tears. The words of these songs were so emotive and had a special significance for the children at Braithwaite, who all had to make Herculean efforts to achieve their own personal goals.

Another event not to be missed was the school Sports Day when, once again, all the children were encouraged to take part. Pete was always keen to join in any event that involved throwing balls, hoops or beanbags, as it was a rare occurrence for him to be able to throw to his heart's content without getting into trouble!

He usually took part in at least one running event and I will never forget one such occasion. Pete had lined up with a number of other children, ready to start a race of about 200 metres. When the whistle blew, he set off at a surprisingly cracking pace. Although he was not in the lead, he was doing well and we were all cheering him on, shouting encouragement to him as he ran down the gentle slope towards the finishing line.

About halfway down the course, he looked over his shoulder. Seeing his friend Liz struggling along behind him with some difficulty, he turned round, ran back to her and held her hand all the way to the end. I was so proud of him I could have burst and no medal or cup would have made me more so.

Of course, there were lots of times when feeling proud of him was not in the picture. Parents' evenings were always a trial to be endured and no matter how tactfully the teachers couched their remarks, it was obvious that Pete could be a real pain when he wanted to be.

His behaviour would always get in the way of his achievements and he frequently let himself down. It was as if he couldn't help himself, no matter what threat of punishment there might be. Some of the staff fared worse than others and must have dreaded having him in their classes.

On one occasion he decided to climb onto the teacher's desk and having done so, refused all entreaties to move. Understandably losing patience, the teacher sent another child to fetch Trish Pearson (by then the headmistress) to see if she could move him.

As soon as she walked through the door of the classroom, Pete sat up, beamed at her and slid down from the table. 'Hello, Mrs. Pearson,' he greeted her, 'I was just having a rest!' I know that Trish found difficulty in keeping her face straight but it's another example of how irritating he could be and how he liked manipulating people.

Looking back through his home/school diaries, I found a very good example of Pete's cheeky sense of humour. The teacher had written a couple of sentences about what they had done that day at school and left space for him to copy them underneath. He had made a very poor, almost illegible effort and in red ink she had written 'Silly writing, Peter' and drawn a sad face.

Directly below, Pete had copied this comment in copperplate handwriting and finished it off with a beautifully drawn, smiley face.

I have great sympathy for that teacher but I did have to laugh when I read it.

Another time, a member of staff made a tape recording of Peter making silly noises and later played it back to him, in the hope of embarrassing him. This of course backfired, as Peter thought it hugely entertaining and wanted to know if he could borrow the tape to play at home!

He had an obsession about 'borrowing' things and this could range from other people's clothing, through school chalk and pencils, to videos and tapes. Once, he 'borrowed' a Barry White record, which he tried to smuggle out of school by hiding it down the front of his shorts. Not surprisingly, this was spotted and retrieved. His teacher at the time commented in Pete's diary that 'Barry White has been rescued – without a scratch!'

He always confessed to having taken these items and knew that he should have asked permission first, which would have been granted at least fifty per cent of the time, but we found it very difficult to dissuade him from doing this. Even now, he will occasionally bring something to 'show' us that he's taken from someone's flat or take things from home to show other people.

The school followed the National Curriculum and Pete had to take French, history, geography and science along with his literacy and numeracy lessons. We were never quite sure how much went over his head, as he rarely seemed able to recall the content of most of his lessons. He enjoyed music and drama, art and P.E., although he could often be difficult about getting changed for the sports sessions. He liked going swimming but, once again, would prove challenging after the sessions, deliberately not dressing quickly enough and keeping everybody waiting. Sometimes, he would not pay attention to instructions in the water, preferring to do his own thing but I think some of that may have been due to his poor hearing.

One day, though, when he was about fifteen, he came home from school absolutely full of what he had been doing that day. We quickly realised that he had been having a sex education lesson - a subject we had only briefly touched on, rather cravenly letting the matter ride until he started asking questions.

It became clear that he had been watching a video about the birth of a baby. Turning to Hannah, he said, "When you have a baby, it'll come out of your fagina(sic). It'll go pop and I'll catch it."

Although we knew we shouldn't, we fell about laughing at this description, thereby ensuring Pete repeated it to everyone he met for the next few days. Still, it was good to know that he did pay attention sometimes!

The transport to Braithwaite was by coach, driven by a cheery chap called John whom Pete liked very much. Initially, the coach would pull up outside the house but after a bit of thought, we asked the driver to pick Pete up near the crossroads, 200 metres away from our house. Pete didn't actually wait at the regular stop, as I thought he might be tempted to get on the wrong bus and end up goodness knew where, so instead he waited by a particular lamp post, a few yards further on.

The reason for this was that I hoped at some point Pete would be able to walk to the pick-up point by himself and back home again. He had been to the local shop on his own a few times, as we had decided that permanently locking him in the garden only made him more determined to escape. He made far fewer bids for freedom once we started to let him out on his own.

Initially, I walked with him to the bus stop and waited with him but, when Hannah changed school, I began to drop him off on the way. On my way back, I would go past the collection point to check that he had been picked up. To make sure he hadn't wandered off on his own, the school secretary would phone me if Pete hadn't arrived.

With one or two exceptions, this worked reasonably well and we gradually reached a point where Pete walked to and from the bus stop by himself, although for a long time I shadowed him without his knowledge. If he was doing something he shouldn't and I had to disclose my presence, I had a string of excuses ready, such as 'I was just going to the shop' or 'I was just calling to see…' As far as I know, he never realised I was following him but I often wondered what local residents thought as I took cover behind a hedge or dodged behind a parked car so he wouldn't see me.

He liked to take a steering wheel with him whenever he travelled by car or bus and these ranged from little plastic toy wheels, through a range of Frisbees, pan lids and table tennis bats, to a proper steering wheel that a neighbour's son gave to him. This wheel weighed a ton and Pete's arms must have ached whenever he took it out. He still has it and although it's a long time since he used it, he won't part with it.

Apart from the incident with the washing machine and tumble dryer, I had another story related to me about Pete, which occurred when he was walking home after school. One of our neighbours had a classic car, which he would often tinker with in his garage. Pete was very interested in this and would stop for a chat if he could see the owner leaning over the engine.

On this particular day, Pete passed the house as usual and saw the garage door open but couldn't see any sign of our neighbour. Possibly thinking that it was not a very good idea to leave the car on view to any passing thief, Pete very kindly closed the door. It was only later that we heard the poor chap had actually been underneath the car and hadn't been able to get out of the garage until a neighbour heard him shouting!

Although Pete enjoyed his journeys to and from school, he could on occasion be very naughty. Once, he lashed out with hands and feet at the escort, with whom he normally got on very well. She would often give him sweets, which we weren't too happy about but which Pete quite clearly liked. We never did find out what triggered his appalling behaviour that day but we decided to make quite sure it would never happen again.

We spoke very sternly to Peter about what had happened and asked him what he thought he would do if John refused to let him on the bus again. "Mum would take me in the car," he eventually replied.

"No, I don't think so," said Andy. "Mum has to take Hannah to school and some days she has to go to work, so she can't take you to school as well. I think you'd have to walk."

Pete's face was a picture as he tried to envisage the journey. "I can't do that," he said, "It's too far."

No more was said at that stage but on Friday afternoon, a couple of days after the incident, I drove Andy to Braithwaite just in time to meet Pete coming out of school. He was very surprised to see us both there and obviously thought that he was going to get a ride home in the car. He was, therefore, very taken aback when I drove off, leaving the two of them in the school playground.

"Right," said Andy, "let's go!" Taking Pete by the hand, he set off for home. It's a very long way from Braithwaite to Nab Wood and Pete's legs must really have ached by the time he arrived home. Andy took pity on him slightly and carried his schoolbag part of the way but nonetheless, it was a long and tiring journey.

He never did cause any more trouble on the bus but if ever he had been even the slightest bit silly, all we had to do was remind him of his long walk home.

Cavendish House

Pete continued to go to Brunswick Road for respite care until he was fourteen when he had to move to a different unit, Cavendish House, which catered for children from fourteen to eighteen. It was probably about half a mile away from Brunswick Road and Pete went there for several preliminary visits before he had to start having his regular respite care. Once again, I was very anxious about the change to his routine, knowing how easily upset he became when his life altered in any way.

The care pattern was the same and the staff went out of their way to make the transition as painless as possible but Pete was not happy and took a long time to settle down. Everyone at school was concerned because his behaviour took a turn for the worse but we knew we had to persevere. The respite care was a real lifeline and the thought of trying to manage without it was too daunting to contemplate.

The logistics of getting him to and from each of the respite units he has attended were always something of a nightmare. When he had his weekly overnight stay, he usually went there straight from school and returned to school the following day. He needed to have everything with him that he might possibly need for both days at school, as well as his overnight bag. If he was staying for the weekend, the amount of baggage trebled. We had to remember any medication that he was taking at the time, any money that he might need for school dinners or trips, plus P.E. kit, swimming gear, reading books…

Generally speaking, we made sure that he had all the correct belongings with him but the diaries from this period are full of comments about missing articles of clothing or items to be collected at a later date.

Several of Pete's friends who had been at Greenfield School also used Cavendish House, so it was also a way of keeping in touch with them. As usual, he eventually became used to the routine, and enjoyed the meals and outings. He was expected to assist with chores at Cavendish and liked to help in the kitchen, drying and putting away the dishes. Keeping his own room clean and tidy was also required but that wasn't a problem to him, as he has always liked his living space to be neatly organised.

Once he had settled down, the routine of going to Cavendish one night each week and one weekend each month seemed to suit Pete. Andy, Hannah and I all benefited from the fact that we could look forward to some time on our own, without the constant pressure of being on duty seven days a week.

Andy and I continued to take short breaks whenever we could and as I was working two days a week for a florist in Shipley, which I really liked, life seemed a little easier.

Pete enjoyed visiting me at work on the rare occasions when he was not at school or in the respite home. He would come in with Gran and Grandpa or Andy and would usually stay just long enough to have a quick drink, by which time his boredom threshold would have been crossed and he would be looking for something mischievous to do. On one occasion, he picked up a watering can and started spinning round and round, turning himself into a very efficient sprinkler system. There was not a lot of room in the workroom at the back of the shop and we were all well and truly drenched before anyone had the presence of mind to stop him.

'Baby, You Can Drive My Car'

Pete was interested in cars from an early age and soon learned to recognise many different makes, with far better accuracy than I ever could. He would know who was visiting us by the car parked outside and would often be found sitting in the car of anyone foolish enough to leave their keys lying within his reach. This is an interest he has carried through to adulthood, but it gave us particular cause for concern when he was younger, as he would have climbed into any car if someone had offered him a ride.

He has an unerring memory for who has owned which vehicles, even some their owners have forgotten. He still loves it if Andy and I swap cars and is constantly on the alert for the slightest excuse for us to do it.

Despite his dislike of fairground rides, he has always enjoyed being driven at speed from his earliest days. Steven Rankin, the younger son of our neighbours from Bingley, took Pete for a ride in his car soon after passing his driving test. They were only gone for a short time and I knew that they were only driving around the nearby (largely unoccupied) industrial estate, so I wasn't particularly worried. It was perhaps just as well that I only recently discovered why it was that Pete came back with such a huge grin on his face that day - Steven had been demonstrating handbrake turns to Pete, much to their joint delight!

Whenever we had friends to visit, Pete would drop very large, impossible-to-ignore hints about having a ride in their car or, at the very least, a chance to sit in it and fiddle with windscreen wipers and lights.

A friend from our Zambia days, Dave Oliver, was staying with us on one occasion, when Pete was in his early teens. Pete did his usual trick of wheedling and pestering until Dave graciously gave in and promised to take him for a ride.

For whatever reason, neither Andy nor I could accompany them but, as Dave put it, he was "not about to be intimidated" by such a young man and, having extracted from Pete the promise that he would be good, they set off.

Pete kept his word and behaved impeccably, pointing out to Dave various places of local interest as they drove round.

Pete knows just how to lull people into a false sense of security and as Dave pulled up, quietly congratulating himself on having entertained Pete for half an hour without mishap, Pete opened the door, leapt out of the car and shot across the road, where he proceeded to open the garage door belonging John and Cathy 'Cross-the-Road'.

Dave reported that his cool and confident manner evaporated, as he immediately had visions of Pete driving off at high speed in their car. As he began to think up excuses for his irresponsible behaviour in allowing a minor to drive a stolen car, John appeared, nonchalantly greeting Dave with the information that Pete often paid a visit to his garage, as he liked the particular colour of his vehicle at that time. Thankfully, this episode didn't colour Dave's opinion of Pete, as he still refers to him as 'a great bloke', although I have noticed that he is less keen to take Pete out in his car without a minder!

Pete was desperate to learn to drive and watched with interest as his older cousins took driving lessons and then passed their driving tests. His fascination with cars included what was under the bonnet and he has never failed to surprise me with his unerring instinct for where the bonnet catch will be located in any make of car, even totally unfamiliar ones.

In the past, whenever we have hired a car or bought new ones, Pete would be the first to find and release the bonnet catch - although he couldn't always manage to correctly support the bonnets on their rods, resulting in some close shaves as they crashed down, narrowly missing his or someone else's fingers.

He loved to wash cars, too, and would always be out with his sponge at the first opportunity, 'helping' in his own inimitable fashion. Unfortunately, he would usually get carried away and end up soaking himself and everybody. Dropping the sponge was a bit of a problem, too, as he wouldn't remember to rinse the grit off afterwards, causing scratches to appear on the paintwork on more than one occasion.

Anyone daft enough to give him a hosepipe to help with car washing soon learned their mistake. Rick Sheard, another friend, was both kind and foolish enough to let Pete help to wash his car and had to have a complete change of clothes afterwards, as did cousin Andrew, after a similar episode.

The worst occasion, though, was when Pete spent some time with Aunty Janet and Uncle Stephen while they were living in Surrey. Pete had behaved fairly well and she decided to reward him by allowing him to help her wash one of their cars. When they had all but finished, she handed Pete the hosepipe and left him to finish off rinsing the car, thinking that even if he soaked himself it wouldn't really matter.

He came in after a few minutes, still reasonably dry and told Janet that he'd finished. She went out to put the hosepipe away and was pleased to find that he had finished the job sensibly, rinsing off all the soapsuds and leaving the hosepipe in a neat pile.

The next day, when they set off in the car to go to the nearby market town of Dorking, the car seemed to be behaving rather oddly, kangarooing along. Pete sat quietly in the back while Janet and Stephen looked under the bonnet, pondering what could be the problem. Eventually, having called out someone from the local garage to tow the car away, they were making their way back home when Pete's unusual quietness must have given cause for suspicion.

After some prompting, he admitted he had used the hosepipe to fill the petrol tank. The temptation to pretend that he was a 'petrol station man' had obviously been too great to resist and he had presumably only stopped when the water began to flow back out of the tank.

When he became a teenager and perfectly aware that the age for learning to drive was seventeen, he began to talk about when he would be able to learn to drive. We had never really explained to Pete about his disability partly because it was a difficult subject to tackle - I had never really come up with an easy way to approach the subject - but also because I felt that if and when he wanted to know, he would ask.

I had never wanted him to feel that he was in any way of less worth than anybody else. There have been one or two people with Down's Syndrome who have passed their driving tests, but it was obvious to us that Pete wouldn't be able to. His lack of concentration, inability to anticipate potential hazards and his poor reading were enough to convince us not to give him any encouragement in that direction. Occasionally, well-meaning but misguided people would suggest to him that he might be able to drive 'one day' but we always felt that this was unhelpful to him and totally unrealistic.

Having taken some advice from a counsellor, I decided to approach the subject by discussing disabilities in general, covering each particular topic in bite-size pieces so as not to overwhelm him. We talked one day about Grandpa being a bit disabled because of his hip-replacement operations. On another occasion we discussed Raymond, an uncle of mine, needing help because of his Motor Neurone Disease. We also talked about children from school who were in wheelchairs or who had fits and he was quite able to understand the concept of disability in relation to people with physical problems.

However, explaining mental disability proved a thornier problem. If I had found the ins and outs of Down's Syndrome difficult to understand when Pete was born, how much more difficult was it going to be to explain it to Pete, in a way he could comprehend? We had talked about his heart condition but this had not caused him any problems, so it was difficult to know how to lead from there on to the fact that he had a disability, which would prevent him from driving.

We lay side by side on his bed one day, when Hannah was out and Andy hadn't yet arrived home from work, and I started to talk to him about several of his Down's Syndrome friends. We talked about the fact that Pete's school was for children who had special needs and who required extra help to do things. After a while it was obvious that he was still not making the connection between these children and himself.

In the end, I asked him if he thought that he was disabled. "No," he answered, very definitely.

"Well," I went on, floundering around but deciding that I would just have to spit it out, "do you know that you've got Down's Syndrome?"

He looked at me as though I just landed from another planet, then said, as if explaining to a two-year old, "Mum, I haven't got 'dancing drums'!"

The question of his disability (or lack of it, as far as Pete was concerned) was mentioned from time to time after that but only if it needed to be. He eventually realised for himself that learning to drive wasn't such a good idea and announced one day that when he married, his wife would do the driving. He's also realised that he can use his disability to his benefit and will occasionally decline to perform some simple task, with the excuse: "I can't do that, I've got Down's Syndrome!"

Aunty Janet once complained to him that the trainers he was wearing were making very squeaky noises as he walked. He thought for a moment and said, "Well, I can't help that, my legs are disabled."

Whenever he does use it as an excuse not to do something, he usually says it in a silly voice, to make sure that the listener understands that he doesn't actually believe he's disabled.

I once asked Pete to describe himself, a concept he struggles with. He always finds abstract questions difficult to answer, so I helped him out by being more specific.

"Are you tall or small?" I asked.

"Tall," he replied. (He's about 5'1").

"What colour is your hair?"

"Black."

"Are you handsome or not handsome?"

"Handsome," - in a tone of voice which suggested I shouldn't have needed to ask.

Having established that of *course* he is tall, dark and handsome, at this point he lost all interest in the conversation and wanted to know what was for tea. **(Plate 7)**

75

← Plate 1
Bathtime in Sharjah

Plate 2 →
First steps, Bingley

← Plate 3
Pete with Hannah,
Granny and Grandpa
at Bankfield Road,
Shipley

Plate 4
The new cub-scout

Plate 5
Pete with Hannah and
cousins Andrew and Suzy

Plate 6
'Postman Pat'

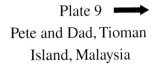

← Plate 7
Self-portrait, with guitar

Plate 9 →
Pete and Dad, Tioman
Island, Malaysia

← Plate 8
Pete with Hannah and
Minnie Mouse, Florida

◀ Plate 10
Entertaining the crowds, Bradford
Diocesan Family Camp

Plate 11 ▶
Catering Department, Craven College

◀ Plate 12
Pete with Mum and Dad at the John
Gaffney home

Part 4

'We're All Going On A Summer Holiday…'

Oh! I do like to be beside the seaside...

Andy's briefly had a job in Harrogate with a travel agency, which meant that from time to time we were able to take advantage of cheap holiday offers. In August 1982, we took Pete off to Portugal for two weeks, staying in an apart-hotel on the Algarve.

Pete seemed very happy to be back in the sunshine and enjoyed the sand and the sea but Andy and I found it a little too windy on the beach, so preferred to use the swimming pool complex at the hotel. We soon realised that Pete, who by this time was walking and running with confidence, would have to be carefully watched, as he would launch himself into the pool at the drop of a hat.

We started to kit him out in swimming trunks and armbands before we left our apartment, so that at least he wouldn't drown if he managed to escape from our clutches. However, as he had clearly not heard the old adage 'look before you leap', there was always the danger of him jumping in on top of someone. The sessions by the pool were a bit like rugby matches, with Pete as a determined little scrumhalf, trying to make his way to the touchline before Andy or I could tackle him!

About half way through our holiday, the running water in the apartments was cut off for some reason and each morning we had to have water delivered, both for drinking and flushing the toilets. There was obviously no water for baths or showers but the staff at the hotel told us to use the showers situated just inside the entrance to the hotel. After our next swim, I took Pete with me to use the showers and having undressed us both in the changing room, went through with him into a shower cubicle.

I had decided to wash Pete first, then leave him to play on the floor while I showered, so that he would be rinsed by the time I'd finished. Having lathered my hair with shampoo so that I could no longer see, I realised I was now unable to feel Pete at my feet. I wiped my eyes as best I could and found, to my horror, that he had gone. I knew that he could not have even reached the door handle, let alone opened it and could only surmise that he had limbo danced underneath the sides of the cubicle.

I was out of the shower in a flash, pausing only to grab my towel and trying desperately to clear the suds from my eyes. A quick glance around the changing room told me that he wasn't there, so, frantically clutching my towel around me, I shot out of the door into a corridor where I saw Pete, naked and dripping wet, with a big grin on his face.

Realising that he wouldn't be able to open the doors at either end of the corridor, I slowed to a walk, intending to take his hand calmly and lead him back to the shower. But just as I was within grabbing distance, someone opened one of the doors from the outside and Pete, never one to miss an opportunity, disappeared through it. Without stopping to consider, I followed, to discover Pete hadn't gone through the door that led back to the swimming pool but had, instead, gone through the door that led into the hotel reception area.

To say that the staff and guests were somewhat startled to see a small, soggy, bare boy running through the lobby with a wild, wet, near-naked woman in hot pursuit, would be something of an understatement. The reception area was particularly busy (we must have hit check in/out time) and the only benefit of this was that the sight of so many people stopped Pete in his tracks long enough for me to grab him.

I quickly headed back to the changing rooms, with Pete wriggling in my arms like a little soapy eel and me trying not to drop him, all the while keeping the towel round me.

After that, I would take Pete into the showers still wearing my swimsuit, get him showered and dressed, then return him to Andy out by the pool, where he was firmly strapped into his pushchair. It meant that it all took considerably longer but at least it saved my blushes!

Funnily enough, we've never been back to Portugal…

Holidays were often a mixed blessing. Because we usually ate out at a restaurant (or in the dining room if we were staying in a hotel), Pete's behaviour on those occasions was invariably good. The new surroundings would usually distract him for a day or two but inevitably, before the end of the week, his behaviour would start to slide.

As I have mentioned, when the children were young, we holidayed in Cornwall each year and for several years were very lucky with the weather. We had some lovely times on the beaches of North and South Cornwall, taking with us a small dinghy and always managing to find a safe spot for the children to use it.

We spent one bright, sunny but terrifically windy afternoon taking a boat trip out to Puffin Island. The captain warned us that there would be a 'slight swell', which was something of an understatement. I was trying to keep calm, so as not to alarm Peter and Hannah, when all I really wanted to do was to get back to dry land. Many a grown man was looking green around the gills as the boat rose and fell with each wave but Pete thought it was hilarious. Each time the boat crested a new wave, he screeched with laughter and the sight of people's drinks sloshing out of their glasses had him in further hysterics. I can't honestly remember whether or not we saw any puffins or seals or whatever it was that we'd gone to look at – I was just heartily relieved when we returned to shore.

After one particularly cold and wet holiday spent trailing about trying to find things to do out of the wind and rain, we decided to try a holiday abroad.

We thought we would start with a brief trip to Paris, to see how we coped on a short flight before trying anything further afield. Although Pete had flown thousands of miles as a baby, he hadn't flown since he was three and we were concerned about keeping him still for a given length of time. I had visions of him tripping up the cabin crew as they came round with hot drinks or locking himself in the toilet and doing who knew what!

I should have had more faith. Both children were extremely well behaved and the tray of food that was served to him, containing his main course and dessert all together, fascinated Pete. The flight only lasted for just over an hour so there was plenty going on to keep them both amused.

Before going on holiday, we had taught the children a few simple phrases of French, which Pete couldn't wait to practise. As soon as we arrived at the hotel, he opened his bedroom window and announced to every passer-by, "Je m'appelle Peter." He told everyone, wherever we went, often to their astonishment and always remembered to say, "Si vous plait" and "Merci" in the right places. His other often-used phrase while we were in Paris was 'Pardonez-moi' or as Pete would have it 'Pardon me, moi!' an expression that he still occasionally uses.

Whenever we went on holiday we tried to book a family room, so that we could keep a watchful eye on Pete. Sometimes this wasn't possible and we would end up, as in Paris, with Hannah and I sharing one room, Pete and Andy in another. Hardly romantic, but at least it saved us from having to pay for new light fittings.

After the trip to Paris, which had gone quite well, we decided to risk travelling slightly further afield for a longer period and booked ourselves a holiday in Mallorca for a week during the school summer holidays in the early 90's. We reasoned that, as it was so popular as a family holiday destination, there must be something about the place that would keep us entertained for seven days.

We stayed in an apartment that was disappointingly basic but the island was lovely. I had expected 'Blackpool with sun' and although certain areas of the island were a bit like that, there were still lots of beautiful, unspoilt parts. We hired a car for a few days, much to Pete's delight, and explored as much of the island as we could manage. The girl at the car hire office really took a shine to Pete and referred to him as Pedro, one of the many nicknames that have stuck.

The weather in Mallorca was superb, there were many lovely places to eat and we all enjoyed the chance to sit on the beach and not have to battle with windbreaks or sudden cold showers. The verdict was that we should repeat the experience the following year.

However, the next two holidays were spent in Menorca, as we had been told that the island was as attractive as Mallorca, but quieter. In general, this was true and after our first, very successful visit when we stayed in a small hotel, we were keen to book again for the following year.

For our second visit, we hired a villa with its own small swimming pool in a different part of the island, which was lovely. Unfortunately the house next door to us had been rented by a group of friendly but noisy young Spaniards who stayed up playing cards, with much shouting and laughter, until three or four in the morning and then slept all day. As Pete never managed to get the hang of the siesta period and kept going from dawn until about ten-thirty at night, we were exhausted by the end of the week and were glad to get home, despite the lovely weather and fabulous views from the house.

Florida

Our first really big holiday was to Florida, where we spent two weeks over the October vacation in 1994. We are lucky enough to have some friends who own a house there and they kindly invited us to make use of it. As with all our holidays, I looked forward to it with a mixture of anticipation and dread. I was looking forward to going to America and the lovely weather (something that I'd really missed since our return from Sharjah) but as we would be sharing the house with our friends for the first week we would have our hands full controlling Pete if he was awkward side out.

After an early start for Manchester airport, the flight to Orlando went well and our friends, Molly and Ronnie were there at the airport to meet us and guide us back to their house. They had arrived in their hire car and we collected ours from the airport, so Pete was, of course, delighted by this. He chose to ride with me in Ronnie's car and Hannah went with Molly and Andy in ours.

The house was beautiful – a four-bedroom bungalow on an attractive site, with a good-sized swimming pool, the sight of which made both Pete's and Hannah's eyes light up.

Despite my anxieties, Pete behaved reasonably well. He shared a bedroom with Hannah, who had the responsibility of making sure that he didn't break any lights.

He loved the pool and especially the alligator-shaped lilo that the little boy next door lent him to play on. We also bought him some other floats and a beach ball, so he played happily in the pool with Hannah and us, or on his own. Pete still did his usual trick of throwing all the toys out of the pool but, because of the mosquito screens, they either bounced back or hit the screen and landed on the floor. It was still annoying, not to mention rather painful, if anyone happened to be in the way but at least the toys didn't disappear off into the distance, which was what had happened before whenever we had stayed anywhere with a pool.

As we were in Florida, we obviously had to go to Disneyland, although we are not really adventure park people. I dislike fast rides and take no pleasure in being spun round and round or twirled upside down and Pete is much the same. However, Hannah was keen to sample everything that she could.

Unfortunately, the queues for many of the rides were very long and the waiting was tedious, despite there being entertainment of various sorts going on all around. **(Plate 8)** The weather was very hot and it could get uncomfortable standing around for up to an hour at a time.

While we were waiting to go on one ride (a fairly innocuous boat trip) we were told that disabled children didn't have to queue but could be taken through another gate to get straight on the ride. We weren't going to argue with that! We were then given VIP treatment, Pete being helped into his seat and having the safety harness fastened for him.

Hannah quickly saw the advantage to this and thereafter encouraged Pete to go on lots of rides that he probably wouldn't have chosen to go on. As Hannah often had to put up with not being able to do things because of Pete, we decided that it was only fair that she should get some sort of payback. Ever since then, though, whenever we go anywhere where there is the faintest possibility of fairground-style entertainment, Pete chimes in with, 'Will it be a fast ride?'

The only ride Peter really enjoyed was one with lots of little racing cars. These were fastened into tracks on a fairly large circuit and were fitted with an accelerator pedal and a steering wheel, which didn't of course actually steer the car at all but gave Pete the feeling of being in control. Pete loved these and wanted to go on them every time we went into the Park (five times in all as we had pre-booked the entrance tickets). Being both a Yorkshire man and an accountant, Andy was keen that we should get our money's worth!

After a week, our friends returned home and we had the house to ourselves. We had tried to organise our time so that we did one big activity every other day and in between just played in the pool, did bits of shopping or visited local attractions. In the evenings, we played games or watched one of the videos that had been loaned to us by the little boy next door.

Pete had never really shown much interest in proper films, so we were quite surprised when he sat down to watch Home Alone one evening with Hannah. As the tale unfolded we weren't quite sure whether this was a good idea or not, as the story, for those unfamiliar with the film, is about a little boy inadvertently left behind when his parents go on holiday and his subsequent efforts to deter two inane burglars. There is a lot of slapstick comedy in the film, which Pete thought hilarious and I had visions of him copying the boy's antics at home. Perish the thought!

Nonetheless, after our holiday we decided to buy him the video and he watched it over and over again. Luckily, the only part that he did copy was where the boy, Kevin, puts on some of his Dad's after-shave lotion, which stings his face and causes him to shake his head wildly from side to side, emitting a blood-curdling yell. This was one of Pete's party pieces for years and he would take every opportunity to perform it.

At the end of our holiday in Florida we flew back to Manchester airport, arriving very late in the evening. The weather was cold and wet; we were all tired and still had a long journey over the M62 back to Shipley.

We took the Shuttle bus back to the car park and found, to our dismay, that our car had one of its windows boarded up. Assuming that it had been broken into, we found a security man who told us that he had found it with the window open, not broken. This puzzled us, as we were sure that we wouldn't have left the car like that. Andy and I both jumped to the conclusion that Pete had had something to do with it but he was so genuinely offended at this suggestion that we believed his denial.

The security guard let us call the breakdown service and Pete was delighted when the AA man turned up in his yellow van, with the lights flashing. After a brief inspection he decided that there had been a fault with the electrics, which had caused the window to open in our absence and had flattened the battery. After charging it up for us, he sent us on our way with the advice 'If you can avoid it, don't stop!' ringing in our ears.

A few minutes into the journey, a window suddenly opened all by itself, letting in the rain and the cold night air. Whatever the fault had been with the electrics, it hadn't been rectified. We travelled all the way home along the motorway, over Saddleworth Moor and back through the streets of Bradford with the sun-roof and all the windows opening and closing like some bizarre, electronic nightmare.

For a long time afterwards, if anyone asked Pete what his favourite bit of the holiday to Florida had been, he replied: "The windows on Dad's car going up and down!"

Singapore

Our other big holiday was actually with the same family, when their son Lee married Jin, a girl from Singapore, whom he had met at university. We were invited to attend the wedding in Singapore at the end of April 1996, so

84

decided that we would make a decent trip of it and stop off in Sharjah for a week, to show Pete where he had been born and to show Hannah where we had lived.

Our departure date was April 1st. All the passengers listened to the pilot with incredulity as he took great delight in telling us about the bizarre weather conditions in Dubai that day – rain, hail and snow. There were groans of relief as the significance of the date dawned!

We flew from Manchester airport on a Boeing 747, which was half empty. Although we had been allocated four seats together near the front of the economy section, the stewardesses had no concerns when Pete announced that he would like to sit, by himself, next to a window.

My reaction, predictably, was that he should stay with us but, having charmed the hostesses with his cheeky grin, they found him a seat within earshot and just about within our line of vision, slightly to the front and left of our seats.

No one else came to sit by him and he behaved really well, coping admirably with the drinks trolley and the tray of food that was brought to him. The stewardesses helped him to sort out the headphones so that he could watch whatever videos were being shown and by the time we landed in Zurich, where we were to re-fuel and pick up more passengers, I was feeling quite relaxed.

A few more people boarded but as some passengers had disembarked, the plane was still not full and Pete was not required to give up his seat.

At the very last moment, a gentleman came hurrying on board and made his way to the row of seats where Pete was sitting. If Pete was actually in this man's place, he kindly made no mention of it and settled himself into the aisle seat. As the plane immediately began to taxi down the runway, we had no opportunity to get Pete to rejoin us.

Once we were air bound, Pete struck up a conversation with the gentleman, who was either Swiss or German but spoke quite good English. Another video started and Peter sat quietly watching that so, once again, I began to relax. His neighbour took out a book and apart from blowing his nose loudly several times, relapsed into silence until the next meal, a full three-course dinner, was served, when he very kindly helped Pete to unwrap all the cutlery and condiments.

I was keeping a beady eye on the proceedings while trying to enjoy my own meal, which was of a high standard for airline food. As we finished the meal and the hostesses came round to collect the trays, they also handed out hot flannels.

Suddenly, from Pete's row, there came the most appalling sound of someone snorting into a handkerchief or no, Heaven forbid, a hot flannel!

Knowing Pete's love of mimicry, I could just envisage what he'd done. Although I couldn't quite see him from where I was sitting, I leaned forward far enough to catch sight of him and, wagging my finger to emphasise my words and using my best Joyce Grenfell voice, said sternly: "Peter Crabtree, you do NOT use the flannel to blow your nose into!"

There was a prolonged silence. Then Pete leaned forward, waving his clearly unused facecloth still in its little wrapper. "I didn't – it was him!"

I retreated behind my book and didn't emerge again until we had landed at Dubai airport and the foreign gentleman had departed.

The week we spent in Sharjah was wonderful and we showed Pete not only the house where we had lived when he was a baby but also the Rashid hospital, where he had spent the first week of his life, and Dad's old workplace. Several members of staff remembered when Pete had been born.

The chap who had previously been Andy's assistant accountant, still worked for the company. He, his wife and their children all made us very welcome and even kindly gave us the use of one of their cars for the week, which thrilled Pete.

We did quite a lot of sightseeing and were astonished how much Sharjah had changed since we had lived there. Finding our house was not nearly as easy as we had thought, as a huge amount of building work had taken place in the intervening years. Our little settlement, which had stood alone in our day, was now completely dwarfed by enormous detached houses.

The first two nights of our holiday were spent in a hotel in town and then we transferred to the Lou'Lou'a Beach Hotel, which was in a very pretty spot. The children were delighted with the amenities but, for some reason, the hotel management had assumed that there were only three of us staying.

We had booked a family room so there was plenty of space but, being the Easter holidays, the hotel was fully booked and every single bed in the hotel was in use. In the end, after a bit of pressure, they found an old folding bed for Pete.

He immediately sat on it to test it out. At once, the bed refolded itself - with Pete inside! We discovered that it would stay put if he climbed on to it very carefully and lay straight down but if he forgot to do this, the bed would close up. It became known as 'the tip-up bed' and even now, if we ever stay anywhere with a folding bed, Pete always needs reassuring that it won't fold up with him in it.

At the end of our week in Sharjah we flew to Singapore, spending a few days at the hotel where the wedding would be held later in the month. Then we made our way by bus to Malacca on the west coast of Malaysia.

We had opted to stay in a small family-run hotel, although the accommodation was actually in typical Malay houses scattered around the grounds, with a bar, restaurant and swimming pool located centrally. It was all slightly dilapidated but there were quite a lot of local families staying at the hotel and Pete and Hannah both enjoyed having other children to play with. Pete was accepted into the group without hesitation and enjoyed playing ball or splashing backwards and forwards across the pool with his new friends.

The local food was delicious and Pete tackled the noodles with gusto, despite the difficulties of keeping them on his fork. He did try to use chopsticks but gave up after a few abortive efforts, having realised that he would soon starve in the attempt. Mealtimes were messy but no one seemed to mind, so I tried not to worry too much, despite Pete's rapidly diminishing supply of clean clothes.

After three or four nights we were due to move on to Tioman, an island off the East coast of Malaysia, which we would reach by bus and then ferry. Unfortunately, we managed to miss the only bus that would get us across country in time, so ended up taking a taxi. This wasn't as expensive as it might sound and we were happily enjoying the scenery, watching monkeys swinging through the palm trees or running along by the side of the road, when our driver suddenly turned off the long, narrow ribbon of a main road on to a dirt track that lead off into the jungle.

Somewhat alarmed, Andy asked the driver where he was taking us, as we bounced and swerved up and down over the rutted track. The driver didn't speak enough English to explain anything to our satisfaction and it was in some trepidation that we climbed out of the car when he pulled up in front of a ramshackle house. "My brother lives here; he will take you to Mersing. Wait here, I will get him."

Much to our relief, another man emerged from the house after a few minutes and started to load our luggage into a different car. I must admit I had been envisaging robbery at the very least, with Hannah and me being sold off into white slavery. I couldn't think what they would do with Pete, as I couldn't see him being a very co-operative slave, so I was profoundly grateful that all we were doing was changing cars.

It was a five-and-a-half hour-long journey from Malacca to Mersing but we must have made up the time, even with the unscheduled stop, as the boat was still in dock. We were told that we had time to buy some provisions for the journey from a street vendor, which was a relief, as we had not eaten since we left the hotel early that morning and by now it was well after lunch time.

I was taken aback to find that the boat was quite old and rather small, holding about sixty people in one long cabin below deck. The seats were just basic plastic chairs arranged in rows, their metal legs anchored to the floor. At the front was a large screen on which American videos were shown continuously during the trip.

It was incredibly hot in the boat, the plastic seating was very uncomfortable and we were all drenched in perspiration within a very short time. We were not allowed to go up on deck and, in any case, the closely packed rows of seats would have made it impossible to move about without causing considerable disruption.

When I had glanced at the map, the island hadn't looked very far away and I was once again beginning to think we were being kidnapped when a slowing of the boat's speed and shouting from above alerted us to the fact that we were rapidly approaching land.

Looking out of the window I could see row upon row of 'A' frame huts surrounded by towering palm trees. I was not amused. Had we really travelled all this way, in uncomfortable conditions, to spend five nights in a *hut*?

Fortunately not. We were told that we would be disembarking further round the island. After another twenty minutes or so we again pulled up to a jetty, where I could see a small hotel, surrounded by some bungalows. This was a definite improvement on the previous resort but still not what I had expected. However, once again we were told to remain on board.

By the time we finally reached our destination, I almost couldn't have cared what the accommodation was like, as I was heartily sick of being on the boat. Pete and Hannah were both fed up, hot, tired and hungry. I think by this time all that any of us wanted was a shower, some food and bed.

What a wonderful sight, then, to find that we were staying in a truly fabulous hotel. The accommodation was in two-storey houses scattered around the grounds, like the ones in Malacca, but these were fantastic, with spacious, air-conditioned rooms.

We were led to an upstairs apartment which would have been big enough for a family of eight and were even more astonished when Pete and Hannah were taken through a communicating door into another apartment of the same size. My good humour was instantly restored and, after a shower and an excellent meal, I think that we were all of the opinion that the tedious journey had been worth it.

The next few days were blissful. The pool had a bar in the middle, which, because it could only be reached by swimming across to it, encouraged Pete's efforts. He was in his element, doggy-paddling his way up to the bar and ordering a Coca Cola or a Sprite.

The weather was very hot and, as always, Pete's skin was burning quickly, so we had to smother him in suntan lotion and get him to wear a tee shirt in the pool. Trying to keep out of the sun in the middle of the day became something of a priority and we were pleased to find a snooker room in a large, air-conditioned bar, some distance away from the main part of the resort. Pete and I challenged Hannah and Andy to several games, winning occasionally, much to Pete's delight.

Hannah opted to go horse riding but Pete wasn't interested at all. He did, however, very much want to have a go in the four-seated pedal rickshaws that were available for hire. Hannah and I sat in the back and Andy sat up front in the passenger seat next to Pete, who had been determined to 'drive' it. **(Plate 9)**

Figuring that he couldn't go too far wrong with the steering, we had decided to let him have a go but he almost instantly swerved off the track and into a flowerbed, causing us to tip up. We had minor cuts, grazes and bruises but were otherwise O.K. Pete, however, was very shaken up and thankfully didn't want to 'drive' any more.

We were sorry to leave the hotel but looked forward to attending the wedding and to meeting up with our friends who would have arrived at the hotel by the time we returned to Singapore.

Travelling back down the coast on a much bigger, faster and altogether newer vessel was almost a pleasure, although the sight of the Merlion, the symbol of Singapore, standing at the entrance to the harbour was a welcome indication that our journey was almost over.

We were given the same room back at our hotel on Orchard Road, much to Pete's delight. It was a small suite, with two single beds in what should have been the sitting room. Pete had been very relieved to find that his was not the 'tip-up bed' but still insisted on checking once again.

Molly and Ronnie, who had arrived during our absence, had a room in another part of the hotel so, having unpacked and settled ourselves back in, we went off to find them. Their son Lee (the bridegroom-to-be) and their daughter Melanie (chief bridesmaid) were also staying in the hotel, as were the best man and several more of Lee's friends, so Pete was pleased to have familiar faces to bump into around the pool or in the restaurant.

The staff were very attentive and we only had to catch the eye of a waiter for someone to be instantly at our side. Unfortunately, poolside service was very expensive so we had to drum it into Pete that he couldn't keep ordering drinks and ice creams. He could wait until we were in our room, where we'd filled the small fridge with these items bought at a much lower price from the nearby mini-market.

As the weather was very hot and humid, we tried to take a rest after lunch each day. Usually Andy and I would sleep while Pete and Hannah played Ludo or dominoes or just rested on their beds, listening to their personal stereos.

One afternoon, rising after a refreshing nap, I went through to Pete and Hannah's room to find Hannah fast asleep on her bed but no sign of Pete. I woke her but she had obviously not heard him leave the room, so we quickly phoned Molly and Ronnie to check if he had gone to visit them. He wasn't there. As we had no idea how long he'd been gone, we couldn't be sure if he was on his way over to see them or indeed if, like Elvis, he'd 'left the building'.

Although Singapore was, and still is, a very safe island, I was none the less frantic about the thought of Pete wandering around alone. Andy was calmer but still visibly anxious. He set off towards Molly and Ronnie's room, telling me to stay by the telephone. Hannah went to have a quick look round the pool.

After what seemed like a very long time, but was probably only about ten minutes, Hannah appeared with Pete in tow, a big grin spread across his face, dressed in his swimming trunks and flip-flops.

"I found him by the pool, Mum," Hannah told me, "and guess what he'd done?" I could hardly bear to think, as the possibilities seemed endless. "He'd only ordered a Coke and a tuna sandwich," she said, "but the waiter brought it just after I arrived and asked who would be signing the bill. When I saw how much it cost, I made him take it back!"

"How much was it?" I asked, thinking of how embarrassed I would have been in Hannah's place.

"Thirty dollars!" she replied, which at the time roughly converted to about £13.50. Thank goodness she's her father's daughter - I would probably have meekly signed for it.

After that, we made sure that someone was on 'guard duty' so that Pete couldn't disappear again. However, as far as we were aware, he didn't try to make a break for freedom again.

The island of Singapore is beautiful and has lots to offer the tourist. We made the most of our time, visiting, amongst other places, the excellent zoo, where we travelled round on a little train that took us in between all the enclosures, allowing us to see most of the animals.

We visited the zoo twice, in fact, first at nighttime, when more of the animals are on the move and, later in the week, during the day when we all had an elephant ride. I was surprised that Pete allowed himself to be cajoled into doing that but it was a very stately journey at a very slow pace. Hannah also chose to have a camel ride but Pete wisely declined that pleasure.

Andy and Hannah also held a pair of hairy young orang utans. Once again, Pete turned down the photo opportunity but was very amused to see his Dad and his sister posing with them. Andy teased Pete about exchanging him for one of the orang utans and Pete responded with resigned good humour.

When we visited Sentosa Island, Pete asked many times if there would be 'fast rides' but apart from the cable cars, some pedalo boats and a monorail that ran round the island, all of which he enjoyed, there was nothing to cause him any anxiety.

Pete also enjoyed our visit to the Orchid Foundation gardens. The flowers, beautiful as they were, didn't interest him but the ponds full of huge Koi definitely did. In shades of yellow, orange and gold, with their wonderful markings, they were a joy to behold. We bought fish food from one of the many kiosks around the grounds and, although Pete didn't want to get too close to the ponds (presumably worried that he would fall in), he enjoyed throwing the food, watching intently as the fish came to the surface, mouths wide open as they fought to get at the small brown pellets.

The day of the wedding came nearer and an air of excitement, tinged with nerves, pervaded our group. As the family Crabtree didn't have a specific role to play, we were pleasantly anticipating the whole event. Although I have referred to the wedding 'day', there was actually going to be a whole weekend of festivities.

The wedding was to take place on the Saturday morning in a Methodist church Jin had attended. A buffet luncheon was to be held immediately afterwards for those attending the wedding, followed in the evening by another small reception in the restaurant at the top of the Raffles City skyscraper. On the Sunday evening we were invited to a formal reception for nearly 800 guests, held in the banqueting suite of our hotel.

We had bought Pete a very smart jacket, a couple of pairs of trousers and several new shirts, along with a couple of ties. These would see him through all the various meals without us worrying about him spilling anything. Although we had managed to have some laundry done while on our travels, it was very expensive and I didn't want to have to send another load.

In one of those happy coincidences that occur from time to time, our friends and neighbours from Shipley, the Dawson family, had been on holiday to New Zealand and had arranged a stop-over in Singapore on their way back, knowing we would be there. They managed to book into the same hotel but we didn't tell Pete or Hannah about it, partly to give them a surprise but also because, had anything occurred to change their plans, Pete would have kept on about it endlessly. It was worth keeping the secret, as the joy on their faces proved when we arrived at the Dawson's' room and Libby and 'the other Hannah' opened the door.

Unfortunately, a couple of days before the wedding, Pete had started to complain of earache. The hotel doctor diagnosed an ear infection and prescribed a course of antibiotics. Pete was also told to keep his ear dry.

Although the children loved playing together, it was difficult to keep Pete out of the pool from then on. Everyone kept a lookout for Pete and any time

91

he showed an inclination to duck under the water, there would be a chorus of "Pete, don't put your ears in the pool!"

It was in the hotel pool where Pete finally plucked up the courage to swim in the deep end, having previously only ever swum widths in the shallow end. At first he held on to Andy's arm but soon Andy encouraged him to swim alongside and finally Pete was swimming off pretty confidently into the deep end all by himself.

He was enjoying his holiday so much that I think he'd forgotten its purpose, which was, of course, to attend Lee and Jin's wedding. But as soon as we went in to wake him on the Saturday morning, I knew that we were in for a difficult day. His ear was still bothering him; he was very deaf and also very tired. We ended up seeing the hotel doctor again, but he could only advise us to continue the course of antibiotics, which we knew wouldn't work immediately. He did, however, give him some painkillers.

Despite the visit to the doctor we were ready on time. Pete looked very handsome in his new dull gold jacket, smart white shirt, black trousers and one of his new ties. We were taken to the church by taxi and arrived in good time to settle ourselves before the bride arrived, looking beautiful in her cream bridal gown, the bridesmaids dressed in wine-red dresses of a similar style, following her down the aisle.

The wedding service was traditional and we sang familiar hymns, so Pete was not disconcerted by what was happening. But, because his ear infection was making him deaf, he was too noisy. He was also understandably a bit grumpy and wouldn't respond to requests to be quiet. I was feeling a little unwell myself due to a slight tummy upset and I just wanted to sit still. I kept having to lean forward to stop him from talking loudly to people, which was distracting for them and us.

However, once we left the church and arrived at the venue for the wedding breakfast, he cheered up no end and was soon seated at a table with a huge pile of food in front of him. The buffet-style reception was fairly informal, the delicious food laid out on long tables, giving us the option of sitting inside or out.

When the reception had finished, we returned to the hotel and met up with the Dawsons again, to relax around the pool until it was time to get ready for dinner.

Taxis had been arranged to take us from our hotel to the dinner venue and we assembled downstairs in the foyer. The plan was for the taxis to take as many people as possible in the first run and then to return for the rest of us.

Unfortunately, the taxi designated to come back for us never reappeared and we thought we had been abandoned. Pete was getting rather tetchy due to the waiting around and was also ready for the meal, despite his large lunch.

After what seemed like a very long wait, another taxi was summoned to take us to the hotel, where we ate a sumptuous dinner up on the top floor with panoramic views of the island. It was a lovely evening but quite a late night for Pete and Hannah. Knowing we would be having another late night the next day, I didn't want Pete to be tired and grumpy.

On the Sunday we spent some time with the Dawsons before they had to leave in the late afternoon. We had a fairly restful day until the evening when, once again, we togged Pete up in all his finery, much to his disgust. Having worn smart clothes the previous day, he was not best pleased to have to do it again and kept pulling at his tie, which he claimed was "Strankling my neck!"

His ear infection was beginning to respond to the antibiotics and, despite the tie, he was definitely more cheerful. He was looking forward to his meal again, as we had virtually starved him all day. This turned out to be a wise move, as there were eight courses. Chopsticks were on the table but a fork was brought for Pete and he tucked in to the unusual dishes with great relish.

The bridal party wore their wedding clothes again and all the guests were dressed in very smart clothes, as this reception was much more formal. Pete waited fairly patiently as we made our way slowly along the very long line to be greeted by the bride, groom and both sets of parents. Once we were seated at our table, he conversed sensibly with our fellow guests. The usual wedding speeches were delivered and the evening was a long one but most enjoyable.

Pete behaved well, possibly because he was awed by the size of the room and the number of people in it. He listened reasonably quietly to the speeches and didn't make too much fuss about having to stay sitting down until the formalities were over when, once again, we shook hands with the bridal party. Their hands must have ached terribly from all the handshaking!

We knew that the flight home, a couple of days later, was going to be a long one, with only a few hours' stop in Dubai. We left the hotel at about 6pm local time, and finally arrived back home twenty-seven hours later, exhausted but with lots of wonderful memories.

Under Canvas

Although we had a fantastic time in both Singapore and Florida, some of our most relaxing holidays were spent on the Bradford Diocesan Family Camps, which were an offshoot of the Bradford Diocesan Summer Camps started by the late Reverend John Potter back in the mid-sixties.

The camps were originally held for two weeks each summer, often near the seaside and catered for approximately 60 children each week, 11- and 12-year-olds on the first week and 13- and 14-year-olds on the second week. They later expanded to three weeks, adding a 'youth' camp and then finally grew to four weeks, with Family Camp.

I had attended the Summer Camps between the ages of 11 and 19, first as a camper, then as a helper in the cookhouse and finally as a 'leader', only stopping when Andy and I married in 1975 and left for Zambia. Andy had also attended some of the Camps as both camper and leader, until work commitments made it too difficult for him to continue.

A friend from my Sunday School and Youth Club days, who had been involved with the camps for many years, suggested that we should let Pete go to one of the children's camps. After careful consideration, we felt that the responsibility would be just too onerous. Although Pete had camped with the Cubs and Scouts, he had only been a few miles away from home for one or two nights, with people who knew him very well.

When we told our friend of our decision, she suggested we should all go to Family Camp. Neither Andy nor I had done any camping since our marriage but we decided that this was the only way we would know if Pete could cope with one of the children's camps on his own.

As the time drew nearer to the holiday and the pile of equipment grew ever higher, I couldn't help wondering what we were letting ourselves in for. Holidays, even in the nicest of hotels, were always something of a struggle and the thought of trying to cope with Pete inside a tent, with very basic washing facilities and few home comforts, filled me with dread.

However, Hannah was looking forward to it and I decided that we had to make the best of it. I do remember, though, saying to Andy that if it rained, I would be coming straight home!

Our friend and neighbour, Sue Pedley, had decided to bring her son Will along to Camp with us and Pete was very excited about this.

The camp was near Robin Hood's Bay, pitched in a slightly sloping field, with a wonderful view of sea and rooftops. Arriving, as we did, on a lovely, sunny afternoon, my spirits lifted.

We were shown to our accommodation, a 4-man ridge-tent, which I'm sure was one that I had slept in twenty years before. We were left to unpack and set out our sleeping bags but as the ground was on a noticeable slope, it was difficult to decide which way to put them. In the end we decided that we could only fit them in crossways, with my bag at the farthest end, the children's in the middle and Andy's by the door, so that Pete would not be able to escape without clambering over him.

Having unpacked, we parked our car at the end of the row of vehicles, well away from the tents and playing areas and joined our fellow campers in the huge marquee that was to be our dining room, wet weather play area, meeting room and concert hall.

The rules and regulations of Family Camp were explained to us, we were given drinks and slices of homemade cake and then met up with old and new friends, many of whom were people from the Shipley area.

An old-fashioned bell with a clanger pulled by a rope, attached to a wooden stand, had been erected outside the marquee and Pete immediately went to pull it. I remembered this bell from my early years as a camper, when it had been used to summon us to meals, prayers, activities etcetera. It still had the same purpose but, on Family Camp, a system had been put in place whereby all the children could get at least one turn at ringing the bell. All the names were placed in a box and each day at mealtimes a few would be drawn out, depending upon the number of times the bell would be rung that day.

When Pete's name was read out, he listened carefully to his instructions. As his timekeeping was not to be relied upon, we assured him (and everyone else) that we would make sure he rang it on time.

It was with great gusto that Pete rang the bell later that day, to call everyone to lunch. It didn't altogether stop him from ringing the bell at other times but we did suggest that if he wanted another 'official' turn, he should try to contain himself.

By the end of the first day, everyone knew Pete. People were very kind to him, allowing him to look at their cars or showing him which tent was theirs. As we were anxious he might fiddle about with other people's belongings, one of us accompanied him everywhere but despite this, there was no doubt that Pete was enjoying himself.

Although the weather had taken a turn for the worse, I decided that we would give the holiday a fair chance and we retired to bed that first day feeling reasonably optimistic that we'd made the right decision in coming to 'Robin Hood's Spain', as Pete insisted upon calling it.

Having managed as best we could to make use of the Portaloos and wash tents, we changed into our pyjamas with some difficulty, trying not to let our wet outer clothing drip onto our bedding. Eventually, we wriggled into our sleeping bags and turned off the torch.

The slight slope we had been aware of when we had laid out the sleeping bags became more noticeable during the night and it was impossible to stop ourselves from sliding downhill. Poor Andy only managed to stay in the tent at all by wedging himself against the tent pole but by the morning we were all in a heap at the lower end of the tent.

It was with some relief that we heard the following day that Hannah wanted to share a tent with some new friends, leaving Andy, Pete and I enough room to turn our sleeping bags round, so that our feet were pointing downhill. We still slithered down the slope but at least we didn't end up in a pile!

The meals were very good at camp, particularly taking into account the fact that they were cooked on Calor gas stoves in a marquee in the middle of a field. The cooks were all soon familiar with Pete and when everyone had been served their food and the cry of 'Seconds!' went up, Pete was always first in line.

We ate our meals seated on benches around long trestle tables, which held about eight or ten people. To ensure there was not a huge crush, we had to go up to be served table by table. Our old friend Chris Clough, the chap in charge of Family Camp, selected who would go first. Pete was keen to be on the first table picked and would often join other families at meal times in the hope their tables would be chosen before ours.

In later years, Mark Allison took over as leader and adopted a slightly different system, whereby he would select one table and then indicate in which direction the rest should follow. Pete would sidle up behind him and mimic Mark's words and actions, causing much hilarity. In the end, Mark gave in to this with very good grace and let Pete stand at the front to shout "Right, we'll start with *this* table and go THAT way!" to huge cheers or loud moans and groans, depending on where his chums were sitting.

He always waited at the front, as Mark did, until everyone had been served, before taking his own plate to receive his helping, secure in the knowledge that the cooks had saved him plenty of food.

Despite the fact that the rain poured down for much of the time during our first Family Camp, we were all of the opinion that we should go the following year, when the camp was held at Grange-over-Sands, or 'Range-Rover Sands', as it became known after another of Pete's mispronunciations.

Hannah soon had her own tent that she shared with a friend. Eventually we let Pete have a tent of his own, which was gradually pitched further and further away from ours as the years went by. Andy once suggested that we should pitch it in the next field, so that we wouldn't be able to hear him talking to himself – one of his little foibles – but we never actually succumbed to that temptation.

Pete experienced a huge sense of freedom at Camp because, although Mum and Dad were able to back off, everyone else kept a watchful eye on him. If he ever over-stepped the mark, someone would quietly sort him out or come to find us so that we could deal with him. We never did send him to

Children's Camp, though, as we realised that he would find it too confusing, after Family Camp, to cope with a different set of rules.

We quite often used both our cars so that we could take Pete's and Hannah's bikes. Also, in later years, when we camped in the Yorkshire Dales or the Forest of Bowland, Andy would sometimes to go to work, getting up quite early in the mornings and returning in time for the evening meal. I did think that he was stretching it a bit far, though, when he got up one morning and flew off to Italy! He returned very early the following day and had changed back into jeans and wellies before most people were up and about. I think nearly everyone thought Pete was either joking, mistaken or telling fibs when he told them that Dad had been on an aeroplane to Italy.

It wasn't too much of a problem when Andy went to work, as there were activities going on throughout the day, many of which Pete could join in with. He loved it when there was a trip in one of the minibuses, although I think he probably drove everyone mad with his repeated questions, particularly when he asked things like "Are you a sandwich?" or "Are you my apple pie?" The younger children thought this very funny, which only encouraged him - but it could be very wearing on a long journey.

Each evening, after dinner, there would be a game of rounders or similar activity, which Pete would watch from a safe distance, rarely being persuaded to join in. What he really did enjoy, though, were the singsongs. Pete loved to feel part of everything and always made sure his guitar was packed into the car when we were ready to set off to Camp. Mark Allison or Chris Clough would tune it and then Pete would strum along beside them. How they managed to keep to the tune I shall never know but they were always very good natured about it and generous to a fault. **(Plate 10)**

The highlight of the week at Camp was the concert, always held on the last Friday evening. Anyone who wanted to do their party piece was welcome to get up and have a go and Pete always wanted to join in. He usually performed something on his guitar or sometimes on a keyboard if there was one available and was occasionally included in a sketch.

He would usually latch on to someone each year at Camp, mainly families with younger children. One year, one of the leaders brought along his twin nephews, aged about nine. Pete would then have been in his early teens. He was absolutely fascinated by the fact that they were identical but was always able to tell them apart - unlike the rest of us!

Pete was desperate to share his tent, as Hannah did, but we could never trust him enough to allow him to do that. However, on the last night of each Camp, after the concert, the children were allowed to have a 'midnight' feast, which started at around 9.30pm and finished whenever mums and dads thought their offspring were getting too noisy, tired or fractious. The children would gather in groups, cramming as many bodies into each small tent as they could, sharing pop, crisps and sweets which they had bought earlier in the day from the Camp Tuck Shop. Pete was always invited to someone's tent, although we had to go along at regular intervals to make sure he was not misbehaving.

Towards the end of our camping holidays, when Pete was in his late teens or early twenties, we tried to encourage him to spend more time with the adults and took him along with us to the adults' marquee, which Pete referred to as 'The Pub Tent'. In the evenings, we would share a bottle or two of wine or a few beers, take part in a quiz or just sit in small groups to chat and mull over the day's events. Pete would join us if asked but I don't think he enjoyed himself as much as he had with the younger ones.

Pete's godfather, Uncle Nick, came with us on several of the camps with his son. Nick's younger brother, Phil, sometimes accompanied him with his three children. Pete was always pleased to have the company of the Denison family, but most especially Uncle Nick, who has always delighted in egging Pete on. This, of course, encouraged Pete, but annoyed me, particularly when he paraded his love of silly noises.

As Nick himself put it in a letter to me, responding to my requests for people's memories of Pete: *" One of Pete's most endearing qualities is his mischievous streak. There is no malice at all in Pete. He knows what behaviour is proper and he knows exactly how to tip it over the edge so that it becomes just a little bit naughty. He takes great delight in it and he enjoys it even more when he has a fellow conspirator."*

Nick went on to say that he has always encouraged Pete in this type of behaviour for three reasons, namely:

1.   *It is an essential part of his character*
2.   *It is great fun*
3.   *It is bound to be mildly irritating, to say the least, to his parents*

Thanks, Nick!

He continued: *"A typical example of this is calling people 'light fiddle'. Pete knows that this is not quite proper. He knew perfectly well that it was a bit cheeky and therefore naughty but when I joined him in calling people a 'light fiddle', it made it even more amusing for Pete. Here was an adult who presumably ought to know better, who was also being silly.*

"When his parents had to try to keep straight faces or to tell him off, Pete had a fellow conspirator who was also being silly and who could share the joke. Pete loved these moments and there is in them such joy and simplicity because he knows that these are silly moments. In fact, he always says 'Ooh Nick! We are sillies, aren't we?"

The word 'marvellous', declaimed loudly by Pete, has possibly become familiar to many of you over the years, without necessarily understanding where it came from. This is another credit to Mr. Nicholas Denison, who has uttered it on many occasions, causing Pete to copy it with unerring accuracy. We would just about have succeeded in erasing it from Pete's conversation by the time we were due for another visit from Nick, when it would be revived once more.

'Yerg' and 'weeg' were two more noises that Nick always did his best to encourage and it would be weeks before Pete could be induced to stop saying them. Even the mention of Nick, or indeed any of the Denison clan, would be enough to set him off, always with a gleam in his eye, as he knew that the resulting 'silliness' would be enough to drive us all mad!

Part Five

The Terrible Teens

Christmas Is Coming.....

The Fountain pub was quite a feature in Pete's life for many years and he particularly enjoyed our Christmas Day visits there. Since we had returned to the U.K. from Sharjah we had always eaten our Christmas dinner on Christmas Eve, leaving Christmas Day free for us to do as we liked. When the children were small they would be put to bed after our guests arrived but before we sat down to eat, so that we could have a relaxed evening. Usually both sets of grandparents would join us, which then left them free on Christmas Day to visit other family members, avoiding the thorny problem of who to visit without causing offence!

On Christmas morning, we would rise early with the children and open presents. Then, after a leisurely breakfast, we would go to church for the 11am family service, which lasted for about half an hour. It was very informal and the children were all encouraged to take along a present they had received to show to the rest of the congregation.

One year, for a joke, we bought Pete a false beard, which he insisted upon wearing to church. He always wanted to show off whatever had taken his fancy from his pile of gifts. We quite often had to restrain him from taking something far too large, such as his go-kart or even the snooker table, which we would find him trying to manhandle out to the car.

After church we would make our way to the Fountain, where Joan, the landlady and her husband Frank, would have a pile of presents, usually selection boxes of sweets, waiting for any children who called. Pete was always delighted by this and would happily tuck into the contents of his, knowing that he didn't have to leave space for Christmas dinner. We usually stayed for about an hour and then went on to visits friends in Shipley, who always had lovely presents for the children and tasty snacks ready for us to share. Pete would always be on good form and would have everyone rolling with laughter.

When we returned home, we would light the fire and settle down to play with whatever toys or games the children had received, or watch a video together. The children would eventually want more food, so we fed them the remains of the previous evening's dinner, which they always seemed happy about.

As they grew older, they were allowed to stay up to eat with us on Christmas Eve, under strict instructions that this was really adult time and they had to be on their best behaviour. Usually, because they were worried that their presents wouldn't appear next morning if they were naughty, they were both angelic. It also helped that there were lots of other people to entertain them until it was time for bed.

One year, when Pete was about thirteen, he joined us at the table for dinner on Christmas Eve but was very grumpy indeed, hanging his head and not wanting to join in the conversation at all, which was most unlike him. Even the sight of his dinner didn't seem to lift his spirits. I knew that there really was something wrong when, after a couple of mouthfuls, he refused to eat anything more and promptly burst into tears. We couldn't get out of him what the problem was but ended up giving him a dose of Calpol and tucking him up in bed.

We kept checking on him during the evening but he didn't appear to have an upset tummy, which had been my first thought. He was unsettled during the night and still didn't want anything to eat the following morning, being only partially distracted by his Christmas presents. He was morose and listless and I was becoming increasingly worried about him. His temperature was normal but there was obviously something wrong.

We didn't go to church that morning and kept trying to tempt him with things to eat but he wouldn't have anything but drinks. I can't remember now who finally worked out that he had toothache. I don't think he'd ever had it before and probably didn't know how to describe it. Once we'd realised what was wrong, it seemed so obvious that I could hardly believe that it had taken this long for the penny to drop.

I drove him to Bradford Royal Infirmary, which for once was fairly quiet. I found a space for the car without difficulty and we made our way to casualty. Although it wasn't busy, we still had to wait for about half an hour, presumably because they had only a skeleton staff. We were then told that as they didn't actually have an emergency dentist on duty, we should go home and ring our own dental surgery.

We trudged back to the car and drove home, where I rang the dentist's number. An answer phone clicked in, with the message that we should ring a different number to contact the duty dentist. It was clear from the background noises that the dentist was at home when I phoned but he was very understanding about our situation and agreed to see us at the surgery, arranging to meet us there about half an hour later.

Having examined Pete's teeth, he confirmed my worst suspicions and said that one tooth would need to be extracted. Because of the hole in his heart, whenever Pete has to have invasive dental treatment he needs a dose of antibiotic medicine, which the dentist didn't keep in stock. He wrote a prescription and told me to take it to the Infirmary where they would have a pharmacist on duty, so I put an increasingly unhappy Pete back in the car and drove back to the BRI.

Once we had collected the medicine, I had to give Pete a spoonful of it, then take him home again and wait for an hour to give it time to get into his system. We then returned to the dental surgery, where the dentist was waiting for us. Poor Pete had to endure a local anaesthetic and then the indignity of an extraction.

However, once the injection had begun to work and the pain had gone, he cheered up noticeably. The removal of the tooth was done very calmly and, although I was really worried that it might put Pete off going to the dentist ever again, he coped with it remarkably well. It probably helped that the chap on duty was not our own dentist, so Pete could rest assured that *our* dentist wouldn't dream of doing a thing like that to him!

After that, we called to visit Aunty Alison and Uncle Granville, who lived just around the corner from our dental surgery. They were very sympathetic and once the injection had worn off and Pete was able to feel his lip, plied him with food and drink, as he was by this time a very hungry boy.

Not Pete's best Christmas but certainly a memorable one!

Football crazy

Andy, for his sins, has always been a Bradford City supporter, regularly attending home matches when he was a young man and taking an interest in their performance even when we were living abroad. It wasn't very easy for him to find the time to attend matches when the children were young but he eventually decided that Pete was old enough to accompany him to the occasional match at Valley Parade, calling at the Fountain pub first for fish and chips. It soon became clear that the *only* attraction of these outings, as far as Pete was concerned, was the lunch beforehand and that he had absolutely no interest in the game at all. Indeed, Pete often complained that it was 'too noisy' and would become quite distressed when people nearby shouted loudly at the players or the referee.

One of Pete's habits, which we have tried to curtail with little success, is to chew his fingers. It's something that he does when he is bored and he did it quite regularly when he went to watch City play. On one occasion, a nearby supporter, who was obviously not very pleased with the way the game was progressing, shouted to the referee, "Get yer finger out, mate!" Pete jumped a foot in the air and complied with this instruction immediately - the only time that he's ever been known to do so!

Andy stopped taking Pete to Valley Parade and instead took Hannah from time to time. She quite enjoyed the matches and had some understanding of the rules of the game but eventually Andy stopped taking her, too, as he felt that the language used by people in the crowd wasn't appropriate. He himself has only attended sporadically since then but I think that's more to do with the quality of the football!

Gourmet or gourmand?

Eating out, as I have mentioned, has always been a huge pleasure to Pete and he can always remember exactly what he ate, in which restaurant, years after the event. He loves to talk about food and will ask other people what they have eaten that day, being slightly shocked if they can't remember. He has rarely disgraced us during our many forays into cafes, restaurants or when eating in other people's homes. There have, though, been odd moments, usually after he has finished eating.

He has accompanied Aunty Kath, Andy's younger sister to several restaurants in Bradford that serve Asian food and, although he generally sticks to the milder dishes, always enjoys what is on offer. After one visit, when they had finished their meal, they left the table and went to pay the bill. Aunty Kath was occupied with sorting out her money and wasn't really paying attention to Pete but when she had finished, he passed her a great handful of loose change.

"What's this for?" she asked him.

"It's for you," he replied.

"Where did it come from?" she queried, having already discovered he didn't have any money with him.

"Out of that dish," he said, pointing nonchalantly to the basket on the side that had, until a moment before, contained the waiters' tips.

I suspect that she never took Pete to that particular establishment again.

We occasionally took him to a fish and chip café in Saltaire, which he always enjoyed visiting. One Saturday lunchtime, after we had eaten generous portions of fish and chips with bread and butter, we rose to leave, having already settled the bill.

As we threaded our way through the tables, Pete spotted two ladies sitting together who had clearly finished their lunch but hadn't eaten all their bread. He stopped and asked them, very politely but in tones reminiscent of Oliver Twist, if he could have the remaining slices.

Obviously thinking that the poor boy had not been properly fed, they carefully wrapped the bread in a serviette and handed it to him. By this time Andy and Hannah were outside on the pavement, wondering what was keeping us, so all I could do was to thank them and then hoist Pete outside before he could repeat the exercise at any of the other tables.

On a visit to another café we were given individual teabags with drawstrings on them, which were then something of a novelty. When my attention was elsewhere, Pete took the opportunity of removing my teabag from the saucer. Having quietly examined it, he then raised it above his head and spun it round on the end of his finger, spraying everyone in range with drops of cold tea. Another café to which we have never returned!

Pete used to look forward to going on trips in the school minibus, which would often culminate in a visit to a café for some welcome refreshment. On these occasions Pete could usually be relied upon to be helpful and sensible but one day, his mischievous inclinations couldn't be overcome and he left the café carrying a sugar basin. Fortunately he was spotted (as he would have fully intended) before he climbed back into the minibus and the 'stolen' article was returned.

On one of our stays at Grandma and Grandad's caravan, we had gone to a local pub with several of our friends who were also caravanning on the same site that weekend. As we walked into the pub, Pete apparently picked up someone's glass and took a huge drink from it, only to discover that it contained vodka and tonic. I don't remember this episode, so I can only assume that someone else made him apologise and decided not to 'grass' (at least, not until now!). I can't think what possessed him to do that but I don't recall him ever doing it again – presumably the shock of finding that the glass contained something nasty was enough to put him off.

Over the years, he has occasionally had a glass of lager and will have a sip of wine for a toast, but he doesn't really like alcohol. If he drinks more than one small glass, he says, "My head's gone for a ride", which I think is a lovely description.

Pete will eat almost anything but he has to eat all his food in order. He'll never load a fork or spoon with more than one type of food and whatever he has chosen first will be eaten before he moves on to the next item. If he has fish, chips and mushy peas, he will usually eat the chips first, followed by the peas and then finish off with the fish.

Both Feet First

It's always difficult to take Pete anywhere and remain anonymous. This is partly because he does quite often draw attention to himself by either being silly or funny, causing people to notice and remember him. The other reason is that so many people know him.

Through the various playgroups, schools, respite care facilities, Youth Club and all the health appointments, Pete has a huge circle of friends and acquaintances, most of whom are happy to come up and say 'Hello' to him when he is out and about.

When Andy and I moved to Hellifield and took Pete to the village church with us for the first time, we went in knowing nobody. At the end of the service two ladies approached and greeted us with the familiar "Hello, Peter, what are you doing here?" They had both taught him at Craven College. From that moment on we knew we would be remembered, next time we went to church, not as Andy and Yvonne but as Peter's Mum and Dad.

We have been greeted in some out-of-the-way places over the years, by people who didn't know who we were but who clearly knew Pete well. Sometimes he would have quite lengthy chats with them without us ever finding out their names or how their lives had connected with his. Afterwards, we would turn to Pete and ask, "Who was that?" only for him to reply, "*I* don't know," in a tone of voice that suggested we were mad to think he would.

Pete has been very lucky with his 'support system' over the years. He (and us, by association) has met some really lovely people, some of whom have become friends rather than just acquaintances. He does have quite good social skills, insofar as he knows how to greet people politely, and generally knows the correct things to say. He usually slips in a question about what car they are currently driving or what type of washing machine they have but other than that, can generally be relied on to behave more or less appropriately.

Of course, if we stop to chat to people for too long, he will lose interest and start to play up by asking silly questions or touching goods on display in shops. So it's never a good idea to linger, unless it's someone who knows him well, who will keep him involved in the conversation.

One of Pete's little foibles is to ask very direct questions, of the sort that most of us would love to ask but don't, as we are aware of certain social niceties. Pete just goes in with both feet, asking questions or making statements that leave whoever is accompanying him red in the face and covered with embarrassment. I have often wished for a hole to open up and swallow me and I am certain that my skin, by now, must be several millimetres thicker than most people's.

Many years ago, I took Pete into a shop that was owned and run by a lovely man and his wife. On this particular day, his wife was not in evidence and the gentleman came up to the counter to serve us, asking politely, but in a very high-pitched voice, what he could do to help us.

Glancing nervously at Pete who, I realised belatedly, had never heard the man speak before, I quickly placed my request. The item that we wanted was under the counter in front of us and the shopkeeper bent down to retrieve it.

As he disappeared out of view, Pete stood on tiptoe, stretched as far forward as he could and said very sternly, "Talk like a man!"

I could have died on the spot. I never knew whether he actually heard what Pete had said but if he did, he chose to ignore it. I paid for my shopping and beat a hasty retreat, making sure that Pete didn't have time to speak again.

That's another place that I never went back to - at least, not when Pete was with me.

He also asks embarrassing questions of people who have changed partner, usually along the lines of 'and how is so-and-so?' (the ex) or worse, 'you're not married to so-and-so any more, are you?' He will often ask these questions in the presence of the new partner, making everyone involved squirm.

He will comment very honestly on what people are wearing or on their hairstyles, regularly telling me over the years that I had 'a head like a boy' whenever I had a style that he deemed too short.

One day, quite recently, we were following a young Indian woman whose hair reached right down below her waist. I was silently admiring the way her thick black tresses shone in the sunlight, when from beside me Pete piped up with, "She needs a haircut, doesn't she?"

Another time, having accompanied Andy to the gents' toilet in a restaurant, they lined up to use the urinals. They were soon joined by another fellow, who broke wind very loudly.

Now, Andy assures me that it is not normally the done thing to make any comment but Pete either didn't know this or didn't care. I don't think that he was too worried about what the chap had done (after all, Pete is world famous for breaking wind) but he was not going to let him get away without a rebuke. He looked directly at the man and very loudly told him to "Say 'pardon me!'"

When Pete was little, I always took him to the ladies' toilets with me, if he needed to go to the loo while we were out. As he grew older, this became less appropriate and I had to start letting him go to the gents' on his own.

This was always a bit of a nightmare, as I never knew what he was getting up to while he was in there. I've spent hours hanging around outside men's rooms waiting for him to reappear, no doubt causing some speculation from the stream of chaps coming and going.

Usually, I would be able to hear Pete talking to himself, which at least gave me the comfort of knowing he was still in there. If, however, all went quiet, I would be in an immediate panic, assuming that he had either been bundled off out of a rear door by someone with evil intent or, more likely, that he was up to no good and trying not to let me know about it.

On the odd occasion I have waited until I thought no one else was in the toilets and then gone to hoist him out, although sometimes I mistimed these forays and would have to beat a hasty, red-faced retreat.

Nowadays, we generally let him make his way to the gents on his own, if we are in a familiar place. If we are somewhere new, one of us will help him to find the toilets, then leave him to find his own way back. He never has a problem with this, having a good sense of direction and good spatial awareness, a fact that has been commented on by several of his acquaintance.

'Alleluia'

Many people from Saltaire URC have fond memories of Pete from the church entertainment evenings, when he would play a few pieces on his keyboard or guitar. He loved to amuse the audience by adding an extra piece, unannounced, on the end.

Entertaining an audience (and hogging the limelight) has always been one of Pete's favourite pastimes and he does have real comic timing. At one Easter church service, the congregation came forward to bring flowers to decorate the large wooden cross. Valerie Jenkins, who was taking the service that day, had chosen a medley of joyful hymns and choruses to be sung as this was going on. Everyone else returned to his or her seat after they had handed over their flowers, but not Pete – he stayed at the front and conducted the singing with his flower, knowing that I was unable to reach him since I was up the ladder tying the flowers to the cross.

Despite these little hiccups, Peter was usually very well behaved in church. After a couple of misadventures downstairs in Sunday School when he threw various objects at the fluorescent light tubes, we decided to keep him with us and he would sit quietly, often with his head resting on my shoulder. He enjoyed baptisms and the Christmas services, and any service where he could take an active role, although he would yawn widely (and loudly) if the sermon went on too long.

It was sometimes hard to know how much of the service Pete actually took in but one year, during the candle-lit Carol Service, the late Pauline Fletcher was reading the well-known prose of Laurie Lee, where he describes the cold of the first Christmas night. As Pauline read about the stars having 'talons', 'ice on the badger's paw' and the ground being 'bitter with stones', Pete gave a huge, noisy shiver. Pauline told me that she didn't know how she managed to continue to read without laughing.

He would often dance along to the livelier hymns played in church and we had to try to get him to realise when this was appropriate and when not – never easy, especially if he was sitting out of reach, which he occasionally liked to do. He would sometimes ask if it was O.K. to do 'knee dancing' or if he should just dance with his arms.

Everyone from church was very supportive and several people have been kind enough, over the years, to take Pete out for lunch or give him rides in their cars. He has also had a good supply of coffee cakes from some of the ladies at church, who were aware both of his fondness for this confection and also that baking is not one of my strong points!

Pete was proud to be invited to become a church member by the Reverend Allan Blue during his time as minister at Saltaire. I wasn't sure how much Peter understood of what went on in church but Allan, having chatted to Peter about it, was happy that it was the right thing to do.

The service of Holy Communion is celebrated once a month at Saltaire, the bread and wine being served to the congregation where they sit, the wine in thimble sized glasses and the bread (real stuff, not wafers) being offered to each communicant from a large plate.

We were somewhat dumbfounded when Pete told us one Sunday that he would be having 'a little snack' at church. It was only later, when we were receiving communion, that we realised what he had meant!

Pete always looked for the largest piece of bread, grinning widely when he found it. One day, shortly after being received into membership, Pete caused stifled laughter by raising his glass, glancing round at the congregation and saying, 'Cheers, everybody!'

His enthusiasm in church was always well tolerated, although I sometimes squirmed when his exuberance caused him to over-step the mark, especially at solemn moments.

Given half a chance, at the end of the service, he would be up the steps, speaking from the pulpit or sitting at the piano, bashing out 'This is The Day', one of his favourite hymns, at full volume.

The annual Toy Service was always held on the first Sunday in December. The children would take in toys that they had outgrown but were still in good condition, which could then be given to needy families. Pete often had toys or games that he hadn't really been able to get to grips with, so he was happy to pass them on.

This particular Sunday was also the first week of Advent and we had been asked to light the Advent candle. Andy, Hannah and I each had a short Bible passage to read, at the end of which Pete just had to respond 'Alleluia!' Being Pete, he couldn't resist the opportunity to milk his moment of glory and his 'Alleluias' would have done Billy Graham proud.

Next, Please

We eventually managed to transfer all of Pete's health appointments to Bradford, saving ourselves the trouble of driving to Leeds on a regular basis. We were in a comfortable routine with the hospital visits, which, although still frequent, were now at least reasonably local. Added to all the other appointments was an occasional visit to a trichologist, as Pete had developed alopecia.

His overall care was at the Child Development Centre, where he saw Dr. Subesinghe, a lovely Sri Lankan gentleman, who was very kind to Pete. Although I often complained of Pete's difficult and unpredictable behaviour to him, Pete always behaved impeccably during our visits to the C.D.C., which I'm sure made Dr. Subesinghe think that I was making up stories with the sole purpose of discrediting him.

For reasons unknown to us back then, Pete was very anxious about having his hair and nails cut. When I wanted to cut his nails, I would almost have to sit on him to do it. It was so bad that we had to stop telling him about his hair appointments. I would just turn up at the salon with him, without giving him any warning. If he did find out beforehand, he would talk about it constantly and drive everyone mad. For a time, I cut his hair myself at home, in the hope that this would stop him getting so worked up about visiting the hairdresser but he still complained all the time his hair was being cut. We started to nickname him Samson, thinking that he must feel that his strength was being sapped with every snip of the scissors.

More changes on the horizon

Although he still had many moments of extreme silliness and some of definite naughtiness, life was on a more even keel. He was still unhappy when Dad had to travel abroad but Andy had no choice in the matter. During the 1990s he was travelling regularly to Spain, France and Germany. Gradually, we took Pete to visit each of these places, which helped, as he could then envisage where his Dad had gone. Andy would also try to ring home to speak to Pete at least once and this also seemed to help him to understand that Dad hadn't vanished from the face of the earth.

But life never seemed to stand still for Pete and as fast as we sorted out one aspect for him, something else would lurch into view, threatening to throw him, and us, off balance.

We knew that Pete could attend Braithwaite School until he was 19, a year longer than for children in mainstream education and it was always our intention to let him have the extra year.

Cavendish House, the respite home, would keep him until he was 18 and we were fairly confident there would be similar provision for him somewhere else. 'Give Mum a Break' changed its name to 'Shared Care' and we were mainly using it as a babysitting service, although we were careful not to call it that in Pete's hearing.

The two sets of grandparents were both very generous in the amount of time they gave Pete but it was a relief when we could use them just to give Pete a treat, rather than solely for giving us respite. They also supported him by turning up to watch him or sponsoring him for his many activities

As Hannah was growing up, she and Pete began to go places together – initially just to the local shops in Saltaire but eventually going into Shipley together, then to Bradford or Leeds, using the bus or train. Peter always behaved well when he was out with Hannah and we always impressed upon him that he was her 'big' brother and that he should look after her. At first, letting them go off together was absolutely nerve-wracking but they both seemed to enjoy the experience and I did know, at bottom, that if anyone tried to harm Hannah in any way, Pete would have done his best to protect her and vice versa.

Changes were looming on the horizon, though, which was never a good thing for Pete. With the approach of his 16th birthday, we had to start thinking about provision for his future. Although he had the option of staying on at school until he was nineteen, as with any other child he also had the right to leave after he reached sixteen.

We were introduced to the Careers Officer from Keighley who had special responsibility for school leavers with learning disabilities. She was a very helpful and forward-thinking lady, who was keen that all young people should have the same opportunities, regardless of their problems or disabilities. She suggested that we should lose no time in looking round the various places of further education available.

Andy and I were keen for Pete to have as wide a range of experiences as Hannah would one day have. The Careers Officer told us not only about local colleges Peter could attend but also about residential colleges specifically for people with disabilities.

A few pupils from Braithwaite had gone on to special colleges and, although the feedback had been sketchy, the idea sounded promising. As always, though, the question of funding seemed a potential stumbling block and we decided that we shouldn't get our hopes up until we had looked into all possibilities thoroughly.

Having made enquiries about local colleges, we both felt that Pete was not yet ready to venture down that particular path. He would be unsupervised for large amounts of time, especially over lunch breaks, and would need to get himself around the college, which opened up possibilities for his silly behaviour to be given free rein.

We spoke to as many people as we could find who had children at residential colleges to get as much information as we could. We identified four possible colleges – one in the northeast called Dilston, one in north

Wales called Pengwern (or 'Penguin', according to Pete), Paduan in Southport, and Weelsby Hall in Grimsby. There was also a place called Lufton Manor near Wakefield, which I think was owned and run by the Home Farm Trust, so we had plenty of food for thought.

The Careers Officer suggested that we should make arrangements to visit each of these places and see for ourselves what was on offer, so we began to set up the various appointments. As Andy was away so often on business, we decided that I would go alone to some of the places. On our visit to Dilston, it was arranged that I should accompany the mother of a school friend of Peter's, who was travelling up for her daughter's first review. It gave me a chance to get the feel of the place and speak to the staff on a fairly informal basis.

The college was situated deep in Catherine Cookson territory, in a lovely rural setting, with pleasant views near to the attractive market town of Corbridge. Sarah was not the only child from Braithwaite to attend Dilston and I saw several familiar faces as I was shown around the college. The accommodation was very good, the range of classes on offer was excellent and I came away at the end of the day feeling very positive about the place.

The only slight concern I had was that Peter would have a little too much freedom to move around the college unsupervised, although the staff pointed out that all the students had to learn to be responsible for themselves.

Having relayed my thoughts on the college to Andy, we then arranged a further appointment to take Peter for a more formal interview. Pete's views on what he would do after leaving school had been hard to pin down, although we had tried to have a discussion with him about it. Apart from volunteering that he would 'like to retire, like Grandad', we had not been able to elicit anything else, so we knew we would have to make the decision for him.

When we spoke to him about the possibility of going to a residential college he made no comment, so we didn't know if this was something that found favour or not.

Knowing we had to present the college in the best possible light, we decided to make a weekend of it and booked into a B&B for two nights, travelling up for our appointment on the Friday in Andy's boss's Mercedes sports car, much to Pete's delight.

The staff at Dilston greeted us very warmly. Pete was made particularly welcome and was thrilled to see his old school friends. The weekend was very successful, as we also took in a visit to Beamish where Pete thoroughly enjoyed being able to ride round on the old buses, as well as eating a substantial lunch in the café.

Although we had been very impressed by the work going on at the college and the obvious commitment of the staff, we still felt that Pete might not find quite the level of supervision that he required and decided that we would investigate the other colleges on offer.

Our next visit was to the college in Lancashire, a much smaller place but with a range of students whose disabilities varied widely. Again, the staff showed a deep commitment and we were made to feel that Peter would be very welcome there.

However, because some of the children were very disabled and the range of courses on offer therefore more limited, we felt that Pete might not be stretched enough.

Andy and I managed a quick visit to the Home Farm Trust place, which we thought was lovely but immediately discounted because the building was surrounded by animals – horses, cows, donkeys, sheep and dogs – in fact, all the animals which scared Pete. Since he had also begun to be afraid of unfamiliar dogs, we decided that it would be too much for him, though they tried to assure us that Pete would soon get used to them all.

The fourth visit was to Pengwern where, once again, Pete knew a few people who had been at Braithwaite. Again, the courses on offer seemed appropriate and we came away feeling reasonably optimistic. The college stipulated that each prospective student had to spend a week there, to enable the staff to assess their needs. The staff were adamant that this should happen sooner rather than later, so we made arrangements for Pete to go back quite soon after our preliminary visit. As we were still planning that Pete should stay on at school for a further three years, we were a little surprised by their insistence that he should have his assessment so soon. However, we bowed to their greater experience and booked him in, only to find out later that they thought we were looking for a place for Pete that year.

Andy was unable to go with me, so Gran and Grandpa agreed to come, as I didn't fancy making the trip on my own. I knew Pete would be anxious and wanted some distraction for him on the journey. Andy had arranged to borrow a car to test drive for a week, with a view to changing his car later that year, so Pete was over the moon when Andy suggested we should travel to Wales in that.

It was with some foreboding that I set off that Monday morning to take him to Pengwern, as I knew he hadn't really understood why he was going. I only hoped that the experienced staff would ease him through the week and the presence of several familiar faces would reassure him. I was to return the following week to collect him and was told that there should be no contact until then. My heart was heavy as I left him and, had I followed my instincts, I would have bundled him back into the car there and then. However, the plans had been made and I felt obliged to go along with them.

Andy was not able to go with me the following week either, when it was time to collect Pete, so Peter's key worker from Cavendish House came with me. It was good to have some company on the long journey and I thought that she might have some relevant questions or observations to make, knowing Pete as well as she did.

I knew as soon as we arrived that things hadn't gone well. Pete had clearly not been happy at being abandoned in a strange place and had decided to be very badly behaved. He had done all his usual tricks – throwing objects at the light fittings and breaking the bulbs, fiddling with other people's belongings and generally making a nuisance of himself at every opportunity.

His worst offence, though, had been to threaten a member of staff, who had shouted at him, with a trowel. Pete had clearly been very upset (although the teacher probably had some justification for shouting) and had lashed out with the trowel in his hand. Fortunately, he had not done any serious damage but the intent had been there and the staff were clearly, and rightly, none too pleased.

Pete was a very subdued young man when he was brought in to us and obviously had not enjoyed his stay. I was very disappointed that things hadn't been dealt with in a better way and would have preferred to have been asked to bring him home earlier, if he was so unhappy. He looked so miserable that I didn't have the heart to chastise him further although we did talk about the incident later.

When Andy and I discussed the matter, we realised that Pete had felt physically cornered in the greenhouse. The teacher had been standing between him and the door, thereby cutting off his means of escape. We had noted before that Pete didn't like to feel trapped and, as he had always disliked being shouted at, we were not entirely surprised that he had lashed out.

We were beginning to think that going away to college might not be possible for Pete but were encouraged not to give up hope until we had visited Weelsby Hall, the last place on our list.

We liked the look of Weelsby from the start and the set-up seemed much more in line with Pete's needs. We spent a long time explaining the types of behaviour that Pete might demonstrate and were assured that the staff had dealt with many students whose behaviour was as challenging, if not more so, than Pete's. The courses on offer were good and fairly wide-ranging and we felt certain that Pete would enjoy several of them.

Pete was offered a place to start in the September following his eighteenth birthday, as we had been advised that funding might not be available if we kept him on at school until he was nineteen. This was slightly sooner than we had anticipated but we decided we would have to accept the change of plan. Forming new friendships and relationships, as well as learning new skills that might one day help him to gain useful employment, were experiences we wanted for him, even if he wasn't yet sure that he wanted them for himself.

We decided to let things quieten down after we received the offer, as there was no point in getting him worked up about something that wouldn't happen for another year or so.

Pete the socialite

Pete was in a good routine; although he was still silly sometimes, there were fewer serious incidents at school. He was spotted throwing stones at someone's window on a couple of occasions on the way home. When I asked why he'd done it, he replied that it 'made their dog bark'. I told him that if they let the dog out, it might do more than bark at him. He must have taken the hint, as we heard no further stone-throwing reports.

Piano and guitar lessons were among his favourite activities and during this period he took a preliminary piano examination, assessed by an external examiner. He received a certificate of which he was very proud and the comments made by the examiner were positive and encouraging. He also joined a weekly Youth Club where he was able to have sessions on a trampoline, which he loved, and to meet up with several friends, although he always complained about the disco music being too loud.

We had employed a tutor for Pete, who came to the house on a weekly basis to help him with reading, writing and number work, sometimes using the computer to produce a neater piece of work. Pete would always make a drink for anyone who visited the house and he obviously looked upon these lessons as social, as well as instructive, occasions. Indeed, if he could get away with it, he would spend more time chatting than working and had a knack of asking just the right questions to keep his tutors from realising what he was doing.

We took Pete to the theatre to see Joseph and the Amazing Technicolour Dreamcoat, as he had learnt some of the songs from the show at school. He was very anxious about going to the Alhambra (the beautiful theatre in the centre of Bradford), which we were surprised about, as he had been there many times to watch pantomimes and various children's theatre events. He repeatedly asked if it would be too loud and we could only try to reassure him that it wouldn't be any louder than on previous visits.

He kept on about it so much that we were beginning to wonder whether we should take him but, in the end, he absolutely loved it. As soon as the curtain rose and he heard the opening bars of Any Dream Will Do, his face lit up and his eyes widened. He sat, totally enthralled, right through the show and wasn't a minute's trouble.

We also took him to see Buddy, the musical show about the brief career of Buddy Holly, as Pete had begun to listen to some of his songs and particularly liked Peggy Sue. Once again, he was very anxious about the noise level but relaxed once the curtain went up and he heard familiar music. After the show, we bought him a pair of Buddy Holly spectacle frames and a video of the show, which he has watched repeatedly.

Having had such success with the theatre visits, I thought I would take him along to a concert to be held in our church, advertised as an Edwardian/Victorian evening. I knew he had sung a few music hall songs at school and thought he would enjoy listening to and perhaps joining in with the singing.

To my dismay, it turned out to be a very highbrow concert by the Leeds Guild of Singers. They sang beautifully but poor Pete was clearly bored and, although he sat manfully through to the end, yawned widely several times. It was a huge relief when they finished and he was finally allowed downstairs for a drink and a biscuit!

The End of Schooldays

As the time drew nearer to Pete leaving school and moving away, my anxieties resurfaced. He was still very immature. I realised that, for any parent, letting their first-born leave home was a difficult thing to do. How much more difficult, then, to let go of a child who was still, in many ways, so dependent on us.

We did, however, get a brief stay of execution. The staff from Weelsby had been in contact with the school and, realising from their discussions with the staff that Pete was particularly immature, had decided to delay his start date until the summer term, after his nineteenth birthday. We were pleased about this, although it did have the knock-on effect of causing a problem with his respite care.

Cavendish House was supposed to cater for people up to the age of eighteen, so Pete would have to move on before his nineteenth birthday. Knowing how much he hated change of any sort and being acutely aware of the huge changes that he would have to deal with when he moved to Weelsby Hall, we didn't want him to have to move to a new respite care home for those few months. Equally, we didn't feel that stopping the respite would be a good move, as we wanted him to be gaining independence from us, not relying on us even more.

118

After a lot of discussion and with the support of his key worker, it was eventually agreed that he could stay on at Cavendish House until he left for Weelsby, but that if there were any further delays, we would definitely have to make other arrangements. We breathed a huge sigh of relief and tried to look forward, as positively as we could, to the end of Pete's school career.

His eighteenth birthday was celebrated with two parties on the same day, in order to accommodate the large number of people we wanted to invite – people who had been involved with Pete at various stages of his life and who had all helped to enrich his experiences over the years.

The family attended in the afternoon, as well as those friends with younger children and some of his school friends, including his girlfriend, Sarah, who must have been at least a foot taller than Pete. He had begun to describe her as his girlfriend some time before his birthday but we had little evidence to support this claim. He was, however, insistent that she be invited to his birthday party and she didn't demur when he proudly introduced her to his guests as: "Sarah, my girlfriend."

We had a break for a couple of hours to clear away the debris from the first lot of guests and then started again in the evening, as other friends arrived. In all we catered for well over a hundred people that day. Pete was slightly overwhelmed and was also full of cold, with a nose as red as the shirt he had chosen specially for his birthday, so was probably not at his best. Fortunately Aunty Alison made a video of the proceedings, which he has since watched on numerous occasions, probably deriving greater enjoyment from that than he did from the day itself.

He received lots of cards and some lovely presents but was very disappointed when he woke on the morning of his birthday to discover that he hadn't grown a hairy chest "like Dad's", something he has always hankered after.

When Uncle Nick wrote to me with his memories of Pete, he mentioned the 18th birthday party, when he helped him to read the speech Pete wrote with the aid of John Bell, his home tutor. The words were Pete's own, with John's suggestions about the sort of things he should mention. Nick helped him to rehearse and then assisted him with reading it out at the afternoon party, when grandparents and family members were there. The speech went down well and reduced a good number of those present to tears, including me.

We attended the Leavers' Assembly at Braithwaite School with very mixed feelings. In some ways, we would have liked him to stay there forever – safe and happy, surrounded by staff and pupils who knew him well. But we were aware that it was time for him to move on and widen his horizons.

After nearly eight years at the school, during which time he had made an impact on all those he had come into contact with, we didn't feel that he could bow out *too* quietly. After some thought, we arranged a small farewell gift for him to present to the headmistress at the assembly.

Several pupils were leaving after the Easter holiday and they were called out to stand at the front of the hall while Mrs. Pearson said a few words about each of them.

When it came to Pete's turn, he waited quietly until she had finished and then handed her the package we had prepared.

Trish could hardly speak for laughing when she unwrapped the parcel and saw what it contained. It brought the house down and seemed a fitting finale for the boy who mainly tried, but often failed, to be good.

The gift he presented was a silver cup engraved with the words "The Peter Crabtree Award for Best Behaviour".

Part Six

College Boy

Weelsby Hall

On Wednesday, April 22nd 1998, we took Pete and a huge new suitcase, a small T.V. and video player, his guitar and keyboard, to Weelsby College. It had been arranged that we would not return for three weeks, to give him chance to settle in.

After the debacle at Pengwern, I was very anxious but the staff assured us that all would be well. They had been in regular contact with Braithwaite School and we had given them lots of information about Pete and the sort of behaviour he might display So once again, heart in mouth, I left them to get on with it.

It was a very strange three weeks for us. Pete had only ever been apart from us for the occasional week. Not to see him for so long was very peculiar. Firstly, I was aware of how quiet the house was. I could no longer hear his voice chuntering away in the background. I didn't have to keep going upstairs to ask him to turn down the volume on his television, guitar, keyboard or stereo.

Secondly, I no longer needed eyes in the back of my head. It was really strange, not having to be on constant alert for signs or sounds of misdoings. My ears were straining in silence, only for me to realise that there wasn't anything to listen out for.

Andy was very busy at work so Hannah and I, for the first time, were able to do all kinds of things together at the drop of a hat. Being able to come and go without considering Pete's needs first was something of a revelation. You thought of something you wanted to do and then you went and did it. Fantastic!

Underlying this newfound freedom was, of course, a nagging anxiety about how Pete was coping without us. The temptation to telephone Weelsby Hall was great but I resisted. I made plans to take Gran and Grandpa with me to collect him on the designated Friday, so that they could see where he was staying. I think they were nearly as anxious as I was and as keen to see him.

We had arranged to collect him just after lunch on the Friday and he was to spend the weekend with us, returning to Weelsby on the Sunday evening. As soon as I arrived my antennae, always on the alert, picked up from the atmosphere that all had not gone smoothly.

Pete had once again given full range to his powers of disruption – taking down some very large framed pictures from the walls, rearranging furniture, trying to wash someone's car with a bucket of cold water and a sweeping brush – the list seemed to go on and on. We had a lengthy discussion, during which I politely pointed out the fact that we had warned them about his behaviour and promised to speak to him about it over the weekend.

Pete was very pleased to see Gran and Grandpa and was also overjoyed to be coming home for the weekend. He must have thought we had abandoned him, his relief was so great. The weekend passed quickly in a flurry of activity and it seemed no time at all before Andy was stowing Pete's weekend bag in the car, ready for the drive back to Grimsby.

During that term, we got into a routine of collecting Pete once a fortnight, for the weekend. I would often be invited to have lunch in the college dining room and Pete was always happy about this. The food was excellent and Pete was probably at his most relaxed at meal times.

He shared a room in college with some other young men but I don't think he was very happy with that arrangement. Having always had his own room at home, and almost always at the various respite homes, he found it very difficult to share his space with other people. Having nowhere to go where he could please himself, watch what he wanted on his T.V. or listen to his music, was probably a form of torture for him. I was hopeful that, after the summer holidays, a place would be found for him in one of the houses.

We met many of the staff on our visits to the college and were always made to feel very welcome. It was clear that, as usual, Pete had charmed many of them but definitely got under the skin of one or two. He had a wide and varied range of courses to attend, most of which he enjoyed. But he clearly found the evenings, and weekends when he didn't come home, difficult to cope with.

Many of the students were considerably more able than Peter. He seemed to be on the edge of any group that met in the students' common room, where there was a snooker table and a jukebox, both of which Pete liked. He did have an occasional game of snooker or pool and he quickly found out how the jukebox worked. He developed a liking for a song called Barbie Girl by Aqua. He played it over and over again, to the amusement of some and the annoyance of others.

Free time, to Pete, has always been a mixed blessing. I have mentioned that he enjoys spending time on his own listening to and playing music, or watching his videos, but when he tires of doing those things he finds time hard to fill. Not being able to read easily, he can't sit down with a book or a magazine, nor readily use a computer. To gain attention, and thereby some diversion, he often resorts to silly behaviour of the type that can't be ignored.

Over the month-long summer holidays we tried to live life as normally as possible, visiting family, friends and neighbours. As well as our usual week at Family Camp, we took a holiday in Somerset, staying on this occasion not with Uncle Nick but with some other friends, Audrey and her husband Rick, who also likes to encourage Pete's sense of fun.

Unfortunately, while in Pete's presence, Rick used the word 'bloody', with some emphasis. As we had always tried to impress upon Pete that swearing was not something we should do, especially in public, he was quick to notice this and to chastise Rick for his language. He has never forgotten this episode and delights in telling people about 'our friend Rick – the one who says "B****y!"'

We had an enjoyable few days with them, visiting Nick and his family and generally allowing Pete a bit of space. When we returned home, I was rather cross to discover that Pete had left his coat behind, a new anorak he would need when he returned to college. Pete often leaves one of his possessions behind when we go to see friends, which we think he does on purpose to ensure that he'll need another visit to retrieve it!

I gave him a fairly lengthy ear bashing and then telephoned Rick and Audrey to ask if they had found his coat. Audrey reassured me that she had, indeed, found Pete's coat and had already parcelled it up, ready to post back to us. I was in the middle of telling her how sorry I was for Pete having put her to this trouble when she interrupted me with a laugh. "It's all right," she said, "I was going to have to post back the jacket you left, anyway!" Mother wrong-footed again!

Before Pete returned to college, we spoke with him about the reasons it was important for him to go there and why he should try to curb his behaviour. It was difficult to get out of him just how he felt about being there or what he might want to do instead.

He presumably thought it unfair that Hannah should stay at home when he had to go to college, and began to treat her differently. Having mostly been very loving, apart from the occasional altercation, he became extremely unfriendly towards her, often snarling at her when she spoke to him and not wanting to hug her when he was ready to leave.

I was quite disappointed to find that Peter would still be living in the main college hall of residence when he returned to Weelsby in September. However, we re-established the pattern of weekends at home once a fortnight and crossed our fingers that he would eventually settle down, as he had when changing respite units and schools.

There was some evidence of this when I attended his review in December but there were still some major issues to address. He had begun to throw things out of his bedroom window, twice causing very costly damage to cars parked below. He could also be very stubborn at times, refusing to answer people when they spoke to him.

On the positive side, he was enjoying most of the courses he was taking and had begun to have guitar and keyboard lessons, which he really liked. He had been out shopping with a member of staff to buy new clothes for his review and was very proud of the royal blue shirt and dark blue patterned tie he had chosen.

I visited the college again with Gran in tow, to watch the Christmas concert, which was held at a theatre in Grimsby. The weather was foul and the drive home was little short of a nightmare, as the fog that rolled in off the North Sea enveloped us completely for miles. However, we both enjoyed seeing Pete perform beautifully and very sensibly on his keyboard.

Pete came home for two weeks at Christmas, which again seemed to fly by. He returned to Weelsby Hall in January and for a while, we went back to the usual routine. However, after a phone call from a senior tutor, it was decided to use the visits home as a 'reward' for improved behaviour, as she felt Pete needed this incentive.

We didn't see Pete for about four weeks, as he blotted his copybook each week by misbehaviour. I think we suffered as much as he did and it was also difficult for us to make plans, as we never knew until the night before whether we had to pick Pete up or not.

One Thursday, when we were told on the telephone that Pete had yet again failed to 'earn' his weekend home, Andy asked to have a word with him, to see if he could find out from him why he had behaved so badly. He spent quite a while chatting to Pete but, getting no sense out of him, ended up by giving him a bit of a dressing down. After listening to his Dad telling him off for a minute or two, Pete must have decided that he'd heard enough and hung up. He would not be induced to come to the phone again on that occasion and, indeed, refused to speak to anybody, even Gran, on the telephone for several years after that.

Andy was still working incredibly long hours as his company was in the process of being taken over by an American group who called him at all hours requesting information which they wanted 'A.S.A.P'. Hannah and I were still spending a lot of time together – attending a weekly keep-fit class, singing in a group at church and writing songs together, so from that point of view it was a lovely time. If I hadn't been so worried about Pete, and Andy hadn't been so busy, it would have been idyllic.

I went across to Weelsby for another review early in the spring term, when it was suggested that Pete might be suffering from Attention Deficit Hyperactivity Disorder (A.D.H.D.), for which he could be prescribed the drug Ritalin. We had always thought that Pete had another condition besides the Down's Syndrome, as he was very different in lots of ways from other people with Down's but I was not totally convinced about the A.D.H.D.

Although it is not right to generalise too much, many people with Down's Syndrome *do* show similar characteristics. They are often perceived as being happy, loving and lovable people, with a bit of a stubborn streak and a strong

126

sense of fun. Like the rest of the human race, there are huge differences between each person with Down's but it is easy to see why the general public categorize them in this way.

Whilst Pete has shown some of the 'typical' traits of a person with Down's, he has also shown lots of other types of behaviour. Many of these have been similar to those displayed by people with autism, such as repetitive behaviour. He has also exhibited much more challenging behaviour than would usually be seen in a person with Down's Syndrome.

However, having spoken to Andy, I agreed they could try Ritalin in the hope that it might calm Peter down so that he could concentrate more easily. We abandoned using weekends home as a 'carrot' but there was a definite feeling that if the Ritalin didn't work, we would have to think very hard about what would be in Pete's best interests for the future.

By Easter, it had become clear that the Ritalin was making little or no difference. We were told by the college administrator that funding for Peter's education would be withdrawn, probably with immediate effect, as they could not show that Peter was gaining enough benefit from being at college.

Although I agreed with this decision in many ways, I realised that Peter could not have his life turned round again, almost overnight, without having any new provision in place. We fought, and won, a hard battle with the funding body to keep Peter at Weelsby until the end of the summer term, so that we could find a place for him at a local college and get respite care set up again.

When Pete returned to Weelsby in the full knowledge that it would be his last term there, he was immediately more relaxed. He was also given a place in one of the houses off campus and his behaviour improved dramatically, as I had thought it would. Although it would have been tempting to push for a change of heart from the funding body, we decided to go along with the decision that had been made. With this in mind Lesley Latham, a social worker based in Shipley, went to meet Pete to see if she could help us to formulate some sort of plan for his future.

Once again we did the rounds of the local colleges and found Craven College at Skipton had the most to offer, both in terms of courses and appropriate supervision. However, Pete would not be attending full time and I quickly realised the implications that this would have on my job.

Finding suitable respite care was another hurdle, as the provision for all users had been decreased during the sixteen months that Pete had been at Weelsby. He was offered a place at Weaver Court, a lovely purpose-built respite and residential home, but we were told that he would only be able to stay from 4pm on the day he went in until 10am the following morning and that this might not necessarily be weekly. Weekend stays would probably only happen once every two or three months.

As we had previously been used to Pete having one overnight stay each week and one weekend per month, this came as something of a blow. On top of this, we had begun to realise what 'normal' life was like and the thought of going back to finding babysitters every time we wanted to go somewhere was not a happy prospect.

'Shared Care' promised some assistance there, putting forward a couple of carers for consideration. As both sets of grandparents were less mobile than they had been, we certainly didn't want to have to rely on them too heavily, so we decided to take whatever help was on offer.

Pete came home for a couple of weeks at spring Bank Holiday and for a week of that time we rented a beautiful converted chapel in Rosedale Abbey. We had arranged for Hannah's godfather Allen Pollard and his wife Pam, to come up to stay for a couple of days near the beginning of the week and then Grandma and Grandad would spend a couple of days towards the end.

The chapel had been thoughtfully converted into two dwellings and the bulk of ours was on the first floor, accessed by a staircase leading up from the ground floor to a large living room, with a dining area and a separate kitchen. The bedrooms were on the floor above, one of which contained a beautiful circular leaded window.

On the day Allen and Pam were due to arrive, Pete watched eagerly from the lounge window in order to be the first to spot their car pulling into the allotted parking space. When they drove in, he dashed downstairs to help with their luggage.

Having shown them where to put their bags, we adjourned to the sitting room to have coffee and there was the usual hubbub as we exchanged news and chatted about what there was to do in the vicinity.

Realising that he had forgotten something, Allen excused himself and went downstairs to the car but, finding that the external door was locked, he popped back upstairs to ask us for the key.

Andy and I looked at each other, slightly puzzled, as we had made a habit of keeping the key in the lock. We started to search for it and then realised that Pete was not with us. Hannah checked upstairs in the bedrooms and the bathroom and we checked downstairs. No sign of Pete or the key.

Each day since we had arrived the children had gone together to the local shop, a two minute walk away, to buy bread, milk and occasionally some sweets or ice cream and we assumed that Pete had gone off on his own, locking the door behind him as he went. We weren't too worried, as we knew that he could find his way there and back and the traffic was light.

After ten or fifteen minutes had passed and there was still no sign of him, we were beginning to feel more anxious. After another ten minutes had gone by, we were seriously looking at ways to get out of the building. The first floor was quite a height from the ground (too high for anyone to jump out) and we were wondering whether we could shout to attract attention, when we heard the sound of a key being turned in the lock.

Pete came in, quite unaware that he was the cause of any trouble.

"Where have you been?" I cried. "You locked us all in and we didn't know where you'd gone!"

"It's O.K." he replied, in the tone of one who can't understand what all the fuss is about. "I've just been to the pub for a Coke and a Mars Bar."

That evening we went to the pub to have dinner. As we trooped through the door, the landlord nodded to Pete as if he were a regular and said, "Hello, Peter, who's this you've brought with you tonight, then?" We discovered that he had indeed visited the pub earlier that day and had stayed chatting with the landlord. Quite clearly, like a lot of chaps when they go to the pub, he had completely lost track of time!

The final half-term passed quickly and it was soon time to collect Pete and all his belongings from Weelsby. There was no leaving party and, although several of the staff said they were sorry things hadn't worked out and they would miss him, his departure was very low-key, which was for the best. Pete was very quiet on the journey home. Although I was disappointed that he had not benefited more from his time there, I had to admit that I wasn't sorry that I wouldn't be making the long round trip to Grimsby any more.

Part Seven

Pete and SID

Home Again, Home Again

It was 'all systems go' from the moment I arrived back in Shipley with Pete. Firstly, we had to get all his benefits re-assessed, as the amounts and types of benefits he could claim had changed because of his altered circumstances.

Being technically an adult, he was no longer eligible to go to the Child Development Centre, so we were invited to attend Waddilove's, a specialist health centre for people with special needs, in Bradford. His other health care appointments remained the same, although were not so frequent as they had been. Encouragingly, the cardiologist wanted Pete to attend for a check up only once every five years.

As he was not due to start at Craven College until the end of September, there was a large amount of time to fill. We spent a week at Family Camp, with Andy travelling to and from work every day. Later in the summer I took Peter and Hannah to spend a few days with Aunty Janet and Uncle Stephen in Surrey. We planned to spend some time visiting friends or having people to stay with us but I quickly realised that we would have to find something constructive for Pete to do, in between.

A friend from Saltaire church, Neil Taffs, came to our rescue with the offer of a couple of days each week for Pete at Shipley Resource Centre, where Neil was then the manager. Several people attended whom Pete knew, so he was reasonably happy about going.

Also, the respite care at Weaver Court kicked in and was, thankfully, better than we had been expecting, as Pete was given three single overnight stays and one weekend each month.

'Shared Care' provided us with the promised assistance – firstly with a lady who had looked after Pete before he went away to College and then, because she was a very busy lady with three children of her own and not too much time to spare, we were also introduced to Debbie and Matheo, a young couple who lived in Saltaire.

Pete liked them very much and seemed totally unconcerned that they shared their home with a large snake. We never did find out what type of snake it was nor if it was venomous but we, somewhat naively, I suppose, assumed that it was reasonably safe. They assured us that it was well-fed and not very active but when I arrived at their house one day to drop Pete off for tea, they announced that they couldn't find the snake, which had escaped from its glass cage. I was sitting on their settee at the time and was horrified at the thought that it might be slithering about somewhere, behind or below me. I declined their offer of a cup of tea and left in rather a hurry, I'm afraid, cravenly leaving Pete to it. They told me later that it had turned up in their next-door neighbour's house and seemed surprised that their neighbour was not too pleased about this.

Hannah was very helpful with Pete during this period and would take him on the bus to Bradford or on the train to Leeds when she had any spare time and they both seemed to enjoy their outings. Their relationship had returned to normal with Pete's return home, for which we were all thankful.

She was brave enough to take Pete into the Harvey Nichols store on one of their shopping trips to Leeds. Passing a lady on the escalator who was wearing a rather large hat covered with luxuriant feathers, Pete burst out laughing and rather rudely pointed at the hat. Poor Hannah was hugely relieved that the lady was travelling in the opposite direction. Another place to cross off our list!

We managed to get through the summer without too many headaches, although I was very conscious of the lack of freedom, which we had so relished during Pete's time at Weelsby. We were back to being unable to go anywhere without checking that we could find someone to look after him and I have to admit, I was feeling resentful.

Worse still was the fact that I had to give up my florist's job. When Pete's timetable came through from Craven College, I realised that there was no way I'd be able to fit in two days each week. On some days he didn't start until 11am or even later, and on others he was finished by lunchtime or early afternoon. I had worked three days a week while Pete had been away and had reluctantly dropped back to two when he came home. I looked at every possibility but there was no way I could perform this particular balancing act.

However, once he started at Craven, we quickly fell into a routine. I had plenty of things to occupy my time at church and was once again called upon to attend meetings, reviews and health-care appointments with Pete, so time passed quickly and I tried to accept my lot with as much grace as I could muster.

Apart from the usual literacy, numeracy and I.T. classes that Pete took at Craven, he also chose to study photography, catering **(Plate11)**, gardening and music & drama at various times during the year, most of which he enjoyed, although he wouldn't take part in the annual concert that the drama group performed, for fear that it would be 'too loud'.

He was still passionate about cars and was delighted when Andy bought an Audi A6, which had heated seats. I think the staff at Craven College were a little taken aback when Pete announced that he had enjoyed having 'a hot bottom' one morning soon after we had taken delivery of the car! Typically, Pete realised that this had caused some amusement and it took quite a while for us to dissuade him from using this expression.

Pete seemed content with his life; we had restarted his piano and guitar lessons and he was attending the weekly Youth Club again. He enjoyed the company of his various carers and would happily tag along with us when we went to social events at church, dined out or visited friends and family.

He still liked to visit, and preferably stay, with both sets of grandparents and one day expressed the intention of walking, by himself, to Gran and Grandpa's flat. This made me panic, as it was about a mile and a half from our house with several busy roads to cross.

On consideration, I was relieved that he had told me of this intention rather than setting off by himself and, after discussion with Andy, we took the decision to teach him the route and see if it was possible for him to walk it. We warned Gran and Grandpa that we were on the way and then I told Pete to show me how he would get there.

He set off very confidently, taking responsibility for getting us both safely across the roads and in no doubt whatsoever about the route. He was very proud of himself when we arrived at Gran's flat and I realised that we would have to let him attempt the walk by himself at some time in the not too distant future.

Over the next day or two we had long chats about keeping safe – only going in daylight, always telling Mum or Dad first, always remembering to cross the roads safely and not talking to strangers.

An opportunity arose for him to walk to Gran's from an Indian restaurant that was very close to the flat. We had gone there for a meal one evening and Pete suggested that he could walk up to see Gran while we stayed to finish our coffee. I knew that he could easily find the flat and when we followed on in the car ten minutes later he was already there, happily eating a biscuit and drinking a glass of juice. He was slightly put out that we had arrived so soon but was very pleased with himself for getting there without mishap.

When, a few days later, he asked me if he could walk from home to Gran's on his own after college that day, I phoned my Mum and Dad to alert them to be on the lookout for him.

My heart was in my mouth when he set off and I think I probably held my breath until Mum telephoned me to say that he had arrived safely. I also received calls from one or two other people who had spotted him en route and had rung me to ask if I knew where he was. This was very reassuring and made me feel a little easier – if other people were watching out for him, too, then hopefully no harm would befall him.

He walked to Gran's several times after that but always rang me to go and collect him, as it was uphill all the way home!

Only once did he set off without telling me he was going. I guessed that he had gone to Gran's and rang her to watch out for him, then I jumped in the car and drove along the route we had walked together. I knew he hadn't been gone very long, so was somewhat perplexed when I hadn't spotted him after a few minutes. I drove back towards home, thinking that I must have somehow missed him, but there was still no sign of him.

Reaching panic level fairly quickly, as is my wont, I turned round and went back to Mum's, thankfully finding Pete sitting on the sofa, quite unconcerned. He calmly explained that he had gone a different way for a change, which was not unreasonable, except he would have had even more roads to cross. However, he assured me that he had used the crossings and I didn't feel that I could be too cross with him, despite the extra two hundred grey hairs he had just added to my growing collection.

Pete had definitely become more independent since his return from Weelsby and was slightly more able to communicate his feelings to us, although he had to be helped with this. Asking him how he felt about something, such as "Do you like going to college?" would most likely elicit just a "Yes", so we had to rephrase any such question to include the words "or not?" This would then mostly produce an answer that was nearer to the truth of what he was thinking or feeling.

His behaviour had calmed down significantly since his return home and, although he still had moments of extreme silliness or stubbornness, we felt that things weren't going too badly.

Pete's Pets

Pete generally accompanied us on the church walks, which took place about five or six times a year. He has always been anxious about large animals, particularly cows and, after his experience at the stables, horses too. As the walks were usually in the countryside, it was often difficult to find fields where there were no animals at all.

He had become scared of dogs, especially unfamiliar ones, after a neighbour's collie leapt out at him through their garden hedge and scratched him. There were often several dogs accompanying us on the church outings. These made the walks something of a worry to Pete - although he usually enjoyed them in the end. Particularly if they started or ended with a meal.

Once he became familiar with the dogs, he would enjoy holding their leads or throwing sticks and balls for them and would always make a point of going round the dog-owners in church asking if they would be bringing their dogs on the walks. He would remember all the dogs' names and would even ask about dogs that had died several years previously, checking if they were still in Heaven.

Pete quite liked to 'borrow' dogs to take for walks with Andy and over the years he has enjoyed the company of Lottie, Crunch and Stella, to name but a few, although he is still wary of new dogs, which is probably no bad thing.

On a visit to some friends who live on the Wirral, he was somewhat alarmed when their large Alsatian, Moushka, appeared. She was only coming to greet us but Pete was petrified and literally leapt into Andy's arms, shouting, "I love you, Daddy!" I was almost tempted to do the same thing myself, as the dog was enormous and advanced upon us at great speed, barking in a way that can seem quite threatening to non-dog owners.

These same friends now have a Giant Schnauzer called Coco, which is large but quiet, so Pete is quite confident with her. Just as well really, as I doubt that he could make the jump these days or that Andy could catch him if he did!

We did have a few pets of our own but I never felt that I could cope with a dog (not enough free hands) and both Andy and I are allergic to cats. So the children had to settle for hamsters (Buddy, after Buddy Holly and Kevin, after the boy in the Home Alone films), numerous goldfish and eventually Twitchy the rabbit. Pete insisted on calling one fish 'Granny' – I can only think this was because it was a silvery grey colour, like Granny's hair, although my Mum never had the orange flashes, as far as I can recall.

On a visit to see a friend of Hannah's, Pete was handed a Russian hamster, one of a pair of tiny, fast-moving rodents that she kept as pets. Pete was completely taken by surprise but to his credit and our amazement, managed not to drop it. I have to admit that I would have been less than thrilled to have to hold one of them, as I found them too quick and squirmy.

As hamsters are not very long-lived creatures, we had to go through several explanations of how, where and why each of our hamsters had died, as well as trying to explain where they would be living after they had died.

Pete really doesn't like uncertainties at all, so we had to come up with a sanitised version of events and try to make sure that we both stuck to that version on every subsequent occasion. He was (and still is) as relentless as the contestants on the radio show Just a Minute, pouncing on any sign of hesitation in the telling of a story. We soon learnt that we had to get our facts in order before trying to explain anything to him.

Pete's hamster, Buddy, had survived quite happily while he was away at college but a few months after Pete's return we came downstairs one morning to find Buddy, inert on the floor of the cage, looking very unwell. We rang the vet's surgery and were given an appointment, so Andy and Pete set off, with Pete clutching the cage on his knee.

When the vet had examined Buddy, he looked at Andy and shook his head. Andy took Pete back into the waiting room, while the vet put the hamster out of its misery. Pete obviously wanted to know what was going to happen to the hamster, so Andy told Pete a small fib and said that Buddy had died because he was old. Pete seemed to accept this without too much trouble and sat quietly, mulling over what Dad had told him.

While they were waiting for the vet to reappear a lady came in carrying a basket. Pete perked up and asked her what was in the basket. She told him it was her cat, which was poorly.

"Has it died?" asked Pete.

"No!" exclaimed the lady, presumably wanting to reassure herself as much as Pete.

With no similar regard for her feelings, Pete said, "Well, ours has!"

We didn't replace Buddy, as I was, to be honest, getting a bit fed up with having to nag both Pete and Hannah about cleaning out their pets' cages. Hannah still had Twitchy, her rabbit, and I decided that Pete could perhaps take a more active role in helping to care for him.

His relationship with several dogs of our acquaintance was improving, and he and Andy had a list of suitable dogs whose owners were happy to lend their pets for Pete to take for walks. He preferred dogs that were quiet and didn't jump up too much but if they liked to chase balls or sticks he was in his element, as he could indulge his passion for throwing without getting into trouble.

A member of the staff at Craven College had two dogs (known as 'the girlies') that Pete was allowed to walk at lunchtime and his confidence increased as he became more familiar with them. Jude, Jack and Millie were added to his list of favourites and he would usually manage at least one dog-walking session each week.

Highs and Lows

At the end of May 2000, we were all invited to attend the wedding of Pete's cousin Andrew to his fiancée, Lisa, which was to be held in a large hotel not too far from where we lived. We took Pete to buy a new suit, which, as usual, had to have about six inches taken off the leg length and three off the sleeve length. However, when he was all togged up in the suit, with a new white shirt, a very smart tie and shiny black shoes, he looked lovely.

Pete behaved very well throughout the ceremony and didn't complain too much as we waited for the photographs to be taken. He was very enthusiastic about the lunch, especially the main course of roast beef, Yorkshire pudding and all the trimmings. But as the day wore on, with the prospect of the evening party looming, he began to ask repeatedly if it would be "too loud".

Andy, Hannah and I wanted to stay for the evening party but knew that Pete would struggle with the noise and the flashing lights, so we had to suss out beforehand where the disco would be and if there was going to be anywhere Pete could sit away from the noise. Fortunately, the bar was to be set up in a separate room, just far enough away from the dance floor for the noise to be bearable. Pete sat out there for most of the evening, with all the 'oldies' who didn't want to dance and kept them all entertained.

Tragically, a week after the wedding, the partner of Pete's cousin Suzy (sister to Andrew), was killed on his motorbike. Tim was a lovely young man in his mid-twenties and we were all shocked to the core by his untimely death.

Pete had met Tim several times and, although we decided not to take him to the funeral, it was impossible to keep from him what had happened. While he'd had to cope with the deaths of his great-grandparents and one or two family friends, they had been easier to explain to him simply because they'd been so much older.

Trying to explain Tim's death was very difficult and although we told him that it had just been a terrible accident, I think that this was the first time he'd realised that death doesn't only happen to the elderly.

We had visited Doris Denison, Nick's Mum, shortly after her husband Jack had died. I had been on tenterhooks, as I knew Pete might plunge in with both feet, asking about Jack and upsetting Doris.

When I asked people for their stories about Pete and received a card from Doris, I expected her to have written about an episode which had occurred on another visit to her house, some years earlier, when Pete had broken their external toughened-glass door. He had been very cross with Hannah for some reason and, as she walked past him to go out of the door, Pete had lashed out at her. Fortunately, he missed Hannah but hit the door very hard. As he was holding our car keys, the door just disintegrated in front of us. I was absolutely mortified although Jack and Doris were very understanding.

Instead of reminding me of this, Doris had written about our later visit, after Jack had died. She wrote, *'You came to see me and Peter, in all innocence, said, "Your husband has died, hasn't he, and gone to Heaven?" I think you were embarrassed and you apologised for him. But you didn't know what a wonderful thing he had done. Most of us shy away from death and don't talk about it, in case we hurt the one who is bereaved. But it made me so glad. Yes! Jack was in Heaven and I knew I would never lose him. So, thank you, Peter!! You made me happy again.'*

Although he can sometimes put his foot in it, on occasions he can get it exactly right.

I don't think Pete would ever deliberately say something he knew would upset someone. He has a very caring side to his nature and has always been extremely helpful to anyone whom he perceives to be unwell or disabled. He loves to lend a hand and feel useful but occasionally he can be carried away by his determination to do good. There have been reports over the years of Pete pushing people in wheelchairs and delivering them to places they didn't actually want to go.

In August 2000, Andy and I celebrated our Silver Wedding anniversary. We had decided we would throw a big party, partly to thank all those people who had helped us out over the years and partly because we both enjoy any excuse for celebrating. We also decided that we would go away on holiday, for a week, on our own.

Although we had managed many short breaks while the children were growing up, we had never been away for more than three or four nights at a time. Andy suggested several European destinations but unfortunately, being a wimp, I could not bring myself to be very far away from home, despite the fact that Pete was twenty and Hannah sixteen.

We finally settled on Jersey, which felt like 'abroad' but was near enough so we could get back quickly if there was a problem.

I had made arrangements for Pete to go to Weaver Court for a whole week, long before we actually booked our holiday. Hannah was already booked to go to the Bradford Diocesan Children's Camp, so everything was sorted out and all I had to worry about was the packing.

About a week before we were due to go, I received a telephone call from Weaver Court to say that they were having to close the unit due to several people, staff included, going down with a tummy bug and that they wouldn't re-open before we went on holiday. I was devastated and, although I sympathised, I'm afraid my main concern was the loss of our holiday, to which we had looked forward with eager anticipation.

When Andy came home from work, I burst into tears and told him that the holiday would have to be cancelled, as it was too late to find anywhere else for Peter to go. Andy suggested ringing round the family but I couldn't bring myself to ask, yet again, for their assistance.

When Hannah came in, she was equally upset on our behalf. I pulled myself together, told her not to worry and said that I would try to think of something but actually, my mind was a blank. I telephoned Social Services to ask if there was anywhere else we could send Pete but, at such short notice, I knew before I rang what the answer would be. In any event, I wouldn't have been happy about leaving him somewhere unfamiliar.

We received another telephone call from Weaver Court to say that Pete could still go if we were unable to make alternative arrangements for him. However, he would have to go into quarantine, which meant he would not be able to leave the building all week and couldn't have any visitors. Also, there would of course be the chance of him catching the bug, so we declined the offer, as we naturally didn't want to run that risk.

The following day I had some errands to run, so I was out of the house for most of the day. Hannah was on holiday from school, so I left her at home to enjoy some peace and quiet, as Pete was having a day at Shipley Resource centre.

When I returned, feeling very low and still with no idea of how I would be able to salvage our holiday, Hannah welcomed me, her faced wreathed in smiles.

"It's O.K. Mum," she beamed.

"What is?" I asked.

"Your holiday," she replied, "you can still go!"

I assumed that Weaver Court must have rung to say that the quarantine was over or that Social Services had phoned with an alternative place for Pete to stay, so I was totally unprepared for what had actually occurred.

While I had been out, Hannah had phoned round the family and arranged for Pete to sleep at Gran and Grandpa's during the week, then at Grandma and Grandad's for the weekend. She had also organised several people to collect him each evening for an hour or two, so that the grandparents had a bit of respite. She had then phoned Neil Taffs at Shipley Resource Centre to book Pete in there for an extra week. On top of that, she had typed out a timetable on the computer, with each person's responsibilities clearly set out in different colours, and had printed off copies for all concerned.

We had a fabulous week in Jersey. The weather was brilliant, the hotel as good as we had hoped and the food wonderful. Pete was more than happy with Hannah's arrangements and I don't think anybody was *too* exhausted by the time we returned. Hannah had enjoyed her own holiday and was clearly delighted by the fact that she had been responsible for us being able to enjoy ours.

The Silver Wedding party went off really well and although Pete questioned us repeatedly about how loud the music would be, he coped very well on the night as I had spoken with the D.J. beforehand and asked him not to increase the volume too much when the dancing began.

At the end of the holidays, Pete seemed to be looking forward to meeting up with his friends and the staff at Craven College. His timetable had changed slightly, and there were more mornings when he didn't have an early start, so on those days I left him in bed while I took Hannah to school. Usually, when I came back, he would be still snoring but occasionally he would be up and about, either having a shower or making his breakfast.

Hannah usually came home by bus but if she had to stay on in school for extra-curricular activities, or if she needed to be home earlier, I would have to collect her. Again, this didn't always coincide with Pete's arrival so in the end, with some misgivings, I gave him a set of house keys for the back door and strict instructions about where to keep them and what the penalties would be if he abused our trust.

Amazingly, he responded really well to the responsibility and was generally to be found upstairs in his room, watching a video or playing his guitar or keyboard, when we returned.

Some friends from church, John and Karen, were to be married in November and we were invited to the evening reception. Pete had been invited by Karen to play his guitar, which he was keen to do, but was, as always, worried about how noisy the disco would be. We promised him that if it became too loud we would bring him home after he had played his guitar.

In the end, by allowing him to sit in another bar away from the disco, we managed to stay until nearly the end and Pete was even persuaded to dance with Karen. He played his guitar very sensibly although, as usual, he couldn't resist adding to the agreed repertoire.

At college, he had added a pottery course to his curriculum and really seemed to enjoy it. He produced some lovely items, many of which we still have, including a plaque in the shape of an angel, which is looking down on me as I write. It is definitely a female angel, with curly hair, outstretched wings, a big, sunny smile and a pale pink heart in the middle of her dress.

Generally, things were going well at college but one aspect was causing us some concern. We gave Pete a daily allowance, which was meant to cover materials he used at college, trips out, drinks and lunches.

Pete soon realised that if he went straight to the café when the taxi dropped him off, he had just enough time to eat a bacon or sausage sandwich before his first class. This was despite the fact that he would usually have eaten a decent breakfast before he left. Apart from him over-eating, this also meant that he had often run out of money by the end of the day.

We quickly found out that if we sent him with more money he just ate more food, so we tried putting the money in envelopes with specific instructions as to what it was for. This had some effect but this problem recurred throughout his time at Craven. I think he enjoyed being able to decide for himself what and when he wanted to eat and the temptation of the café was just too great for him to ignore.

Seeing that Pete's main interest in life was food, I suppose we should have anticipated what his choice of venue for his work experience would be – a week at the Little Chef, which lies on the roundabout near to the turn-off for the Aire block campus of Craven college.

Pete was delighted to be able to work there, and helped to clear tables and load and unload the dishwasher. He wore the regulation apron and was very proud of himself at the end of the week. When we asked him to tell us what he had done, he thought carefully before replying.

"I had a drink, then I stacked the dishwasher, then it was break time and I had another drink, then I cleared some tables, then it was lunchtime and I had burger and chips, then I emptied the dishwasher, then it was break time, then I cleared some more tables, then I had a drink and then it was time to go home." Not a bad day's work, as far as Pete was concerned.

A member of staff from the college accompanied him each day and supervised him while he performed his tasks, so the experience was a very positive one. We were pleased and relieved that things had gone so well.

Towards the end of the year, Pete arrived home clutching a copy of the college prospectus for the following spring term, which he thrust into my hands. On the front cover was a lovely photograph of Pete, looking very handsome.

Overall, things were going quite well. Apart from the fact that he had started to talk to himself very loudly when he thought no one was around, which was incredibly annoying, he was generally behaving in a more mature way.

He had started to attend a social club, which met at The Basement, an offshoot of Shipley Resource Centre, on one Saturday each month. Several of his friends attended and they took part in a variety of activities, including going out on trips in a minibus, which Pete was always keen on, although it was always the driving around that interested him more than the final destination. The trips always included lunch – often fish and chips, as that was everybody's favourite – so Pete was always eager to go, despite the occasional worry that they would visit somewhere with fast rides or loud music.

Pete's 21st birthday was looming and Andy and I thought he might like to go to see the musical Joseph again, as it was being performed at the Alhambra theatre at the beginning of December. We decided not to tell him of our plans, knowing how much he had enjoyed the performance the last time and fully expecting that he would be thrilled by the surprise.

We booked an 'early bird' meal at a local restaurant that was a particular favourite of Pete's and then set off for the theatre. Pete soon twigged where we were headed and straight away asked, "Will it be loud?" We reassured him that it wouldn't be any louder than the previous time.

As we didn't have much time to spare, we just had time to buy Pete a Joseph sweatshirt before hurrying to our seats.

The orchestra were tuning up in the pit and the audience was making the usual pre-performance racket, so it was rather noisy as we made our way along the row to our seats on the second row of the dress circle. We hadn't been able to book front row seats, but they were still good and we were fortunate that the people in front of us weren't inordinately tall.

We had not been in our seats for more than half a minute when Pete started to make a strange coughing noise. This was a noise that we were all too familiar with – a prelude to him being sick. With great presence of mind, Andy (first removing the sweatshirt) held the carrier bag in front of him just in time to prevent the person in front being the recipient of a 'liquid laugh'. Andy helped Pete to his feet, whispering to me that they would be back when he'd made sure that Pete was O.K.

The curtain rose just as they reached the aisle and Hannah and I sat back in our seats, each of us with one eye on the stage and the other on the door.

When they had still not returned by the interval, I was really worried. Hannah and I shot out of our seats as soon as the curtain fell. We found Andy and Pete in the bar, Pete looking very forlorn and Andy just plain fed up. Pete had not wanted to return to his seat and could not be persuaded to do so, even though he had shown no signs of being sick again.

Andy suggested they should return home leaving Hannah and I to watch the end of the show. We both said we would also leave but Andy felt there was no point in wasting all four tickets. Poor old Pete, what a way to end his 21st birthday! Fortunately, we had arranged a small family party for him the following weekend, which he enjoyed, but he talked about our visit to the theatre for quite some time.

Introductions

Just before Christmas 2000, Lesley Latham, Pete's social worker, contacted me to say that she thought it would be a good idea for us to go to look at one or two residential care homes in the area. We had talked to Lesley at some length about our long-term plans for Pete and she knew that we were keen that he should live as independently as possible.

We had always felt that it would be a good idea for him to leave home at approximately the same age that most children do, so that when Andy and I are either not fit enough to care for him or no longer around, he would already be settled.

Throughout our years of membership of Mencap, we had watched as some of our fellow members tried to struggle on to the bitter end, caring for their grown-up sons or daughters when their own health was failing. Usually, when both parents died, the disabled person would lose their home as well. Of course provision for them would always be found, but not necessarily the most suitable and the emotional upheaval was considerable. We did not want

144

this to happen to Peter, and neither did we want Hannah to take on the responsibility of being his full-time carer.

Our intention had been for Pete to live with us until he was in his mid-twenties, but Lesley thought we should be starting to look at what was available, to get some idea of what we wanted for Peter.

An invitation arrived for us to visit the John Gaffney Home, on Toller Lane in Bradford, for their Christmas Open Day. Andy and I went along, not really knowing what to expect.

We were very warmly received, offered drinks and food from a lovely buffet and managed to have a brief informal chat with the manager, who told us to come again at any time and to bring Pete with us. As we hadn't yet discussed plans for the future with Pete, I wasn't sure how to manage this, without him suspecting that something worrying was afoot. However, while we were there, the manager mentioned that the group of carol singers he had booked for the following week had had to cancel at short notice. I offered the services of the singing group Hannah and I belonged to at church and asked if we could bring Pete along on that evening.

Several members of the church choir agreed to join our group to swell the numbers and we went along the following week with Pete in tow. We had a lovely evening, singing carols and other Christmas songs, the residents joining in with those they knew.

There were members of staff on hand, serving drinks and mince pies and the whole atmosphere was lively and friendly. We found that we knew one or two of the residents and Pete was made to feel very welcome and given a guided tour of one of the flats and the communal areas.

Pete asked us later if he was going to live there, so we decided to put our cards on the table and tell him what our thoughts were about what should happen in the future. He didn't make much comment and, as our intention was for him to move out three or four years down the line, we didn't press the matter.

Respite Reduction

Christmas was very soon upon us and we had decided to buy Pete an electric guitar, gluttons for punishment that we are. It came with a large amplifier and we spent huge amounts of time running up the stairs to ask him to turn it down. Looking back, we must have been mad to buy it but he did enjoy playing it and when he could be persuaded to play it properly, could produce a reasonable sound.

Early in the New Year, we were contacted by a member of staff from Weaver Court to say that all respite care was being reduced and they would only be able to take Pete for about three nights a month instead of six. Worried about his reaction, we told Pete that they had too many people wanting to use Weaver Court and not enough spare beds, but he wasn't bothered about not being able to go so often.

Added to this, one of our 'Shared Care' families had cut back their hours, Debbie and Matheo having moved to a new house. While they were still happy to have Pete to stay, it was not quite as easy to make use of them for short term respite, as it was more than an hour's round trip to their new home.

Gran had not been too well over the winter and as Grandad was also not in the best of health, we didn't like to ask too much of either set of grandparents. Hannah was always willing to help out but at sixteen and beginning to have a social life of her own, I didn't want to have to ask her more than necessary.

One or two people from church kindly came forward to help out, including our minister, the Reverend Allan Blue and his wife June, who took him firstly to the National Museum of Film and Photography, followed by lunch at MacDonald's and then, another time, to the National Railway Museum for the day. It was this second occasion that particularly stuck in Allan's mind, when I asked people for their stories about Pete.

Upon going into the café at the Railway Museum for lunch, Allan and Peter had gone to find a table while June queued for food at the counter. After a while, Pete decided to go and join June, who was by this time queuing to pay for the items she had chosen and didn't see Pete come up behind her. As she made her way back to the table, she noticed several people sending rather strange looks in her direction. Of course, the looks weren't actually directed at her but at Pete, who, unchallenged by the staff had picked up a large tray of cakes and was following her, holding the tray aloft like a trophy.

After lunch, they visited the gift shop where Pete decided that it would be great fun to rearrange the stock. With great speed he removed pictures from the walls and demolished displays, Allan and June following in his wake and putting things back. Nothing was broken but, although Pete thought it a great joke, Allan and June must have been exhausted by the end of the day.

With the reduction of respite care, I was finding life very difficult and felt as though we were almost back to square one. This was not really the case, as Pete was more independent in many ways. Nonetheless, I began to suffer a serious depression. The doctor suggested I might like to visit a counsellor. It was useful to be able to talk to someone but the fact remained that we were still as restricted as we had been when Pete was a small boy.

I did begin to feel better after a few weeks and managed to carry on fairly cheerfully but some days were still a struggle, especially when Pete decided he

146

no longer wanted to go to the Youth Club, as he said it was too noisy. That meant we had no evenings free at all.

One day I took Peter into Bradford, to collect tickets for a show Andy and I were going to see at the Alhambra. Pete was going to stay with Debbie and Matheo, so he knew he wouldn't be coming with us. We had barely stepped through the doors of the theatre when Pete started to make the coughing noise that preceded a bout of vomiting and I had to rush him through to the toilets. We made it just in time but I was astounded that he could be so upset just by being in the building.

Pete was becoming increasingly anxious about going on any trips or visits to unfamiliar places, in case there would be loud music or a lot of noise. This was very wearing, as we had to constantly reassure him. Sometimes, of course, we got it wrong and, having assured him that all would be quiet and peaceful, we would arrive somewhere to find a brass band or a loud tannoy system in operation.

As well as his anxiety about being anywhere with loud music, he had started to regularly voice his concerns about going anywhere where there might be large animals. No one seemed able to come up with any reasons for this and I was increasingly worried.

A member of staff who had picked up on Pete's fear of large animals and unfamiliar dogs was addressing this for him at college, where she taught a course called 'Small animal care'. Although the animals were usually the kind that were kept as small domestic pets, the students also visited a nearby farm where they helped to look after slightly larger animals, such as pigs, goats and sheep. There were also some donkeys and small ponies at the farm. Pete was encouraged to go and look at these animals and his confidence grew noticeably.

Various people took their rabbits, hamsters, guinea pigs, cats and dogs into college for this class and the students were shown how to handle, feed and care for them. Pete asked if he could take Hannah's rabbit Twitchy, so we arranged with the staff that I would take it along one day. He also asked if a friend of ours could take in her St. Bernard puppy, which was already as big as a Labrador and he was very proud to be able to assist her with the dog when she visited the class one morning.

All in all, college life was suiting Pete and we were pleased with the variety of courses and the quality of the teaching. The facilities were excellent and, apart from his over-eating (which we still hadn't quite curtailed), we felt that things were going well.

Pete decided he would like to start having his piano lessons at Michelle's house rather than at home and, as she was happy with this, we also agreed between us that he could walk to her house which was less than half a mile away. I would ring her when he was setting off, so that she knew when to expect him; that way, if he hadn't arrived within a set time, she would either telephone me or go out to look for him herself. Generally speaking, this · worked very well and on the odd occasion when he was a little late arriving, it was usually because he had stopped to talk to someone en route.

Andy and I were invited to stay with some friends one weekend. We were going to decline the invitation because Pete wasn't due for any respite care and his 'Shared Care' carers were not free, when Hannah remarked that she and Pete would be all right staying on their own. This idea had never occurred to me and I took some persuading to leave them alone, so in the end we only went for one night, leaving a long list of emergency telephone numbers for Hannah 'just in case'.

I don't think I really managed to relax but we arrived home to find that they had been absolutely fine and had enjoyed their bit of freedom. I was very conscious that Hannah had her own social life and knew that we should not and could not rely on her to look after her brother on any sort of regular basis.

Indeed, shortly after that, Hannah announced that she had a boyfriend called Tom, whom she had met through some friends at school. He was a very nice young man who was in the same school year as Hannah but was just a few months older.

Andy and I first met him when Hannah sang in a school production at Bingley Little Theatre one evening. Worried about the noise levels, Pete hadn't accompanied us so he was very pleased when Hannah asked if Tom could come to tea one day after school.

I had arranged with Hannah that I would collect them from the bus stop, taking Pete with me, as I needed some things from the shop and didn't want to leave him on his own for too long.

Hannah introduced Tom to Pete and then they climbed into the car. I knew that Pete was very interested in Hannah's boyfriend and was hoping he wouldn't tease them too much but, of course, I should have known better. As we pulled up outside the shops, Pete, having allayed everyone's fears by behaving in a very charming and polite manner, turned to look at Tom and said, "So are you going to marry her, then?"

To his credit, Tom just smiled and covered Hannah's embarrassment by saying very calmly, "Not today."

Pete, presumably disappointed that Tom hadn't reacted in the way that he had hoped, looked round again and said, "Well, are you going to go to bed with her, then?"

At this point, I leapt out of the car, went round to the passenger door and hooked him out as fast as I could, smiling an apology at Tom, who thankfully just laughed. Poor Hannah. I wondered how she would ever be able to keep a boyfriend if this was the way Pete was going to treat them.

However, Tom didn't seem too upset by Pete's direct manner and continued to see Hannah for the next three years, until they were both at University and gradually went their own ways.

Whenever Hannah brought home a new boyfriend after that, Pete would always manage to bring Tom's name into the conversation, usually by saying something like, "You haven't got Tom any more, have you, Hannah?" as though she had mislaid him somewhere along the way. We always say that if Hannah's boyfriends can withstand the baptism of fire by Pete, then they must be O.K.

Preparations

We were in close contact with Lesley Latham in the early spring and had paid one or two more visits to the John Gaffney Home, always when they were having a buffet-style meal, recognising that this was the way to soften Pete up. Lesley knew that a place would be coming vacant at JGH and advised us to take it if it was offered to Pete, as she felt that this was the most appropriate place for him to live. There was a good level of support from the staff and plenty of other residents for him to mix with.

I had originally been thinking along the lines of a small group home for Peter, as we knew of several of his old school friends who were now living in this type of accommodation. There were, however, drawbacks to this style of living, especially with regard to the level of supervision that Pete would need.

Although the group homes were staffed mornings, evenings and at weekends, there wouldn't necessarily be anyone about during the afternoons and, as Pete's college hours were so erratic, there would be periods of time when he would be unsupervised and therefore at risk to himself and the other residents. Also, I was concerned about what would happen if he was unwell or when college was closed for the holidays.

Lesley put us in touch with Jeannie McNeil, an Occupational Therapist based in Bradford, who would assess Pete to find out just what assistance he would need. In April 2001 she began to visit us once a fortnight.

The first time she came to meet Pete she instantly formed a rapport with him. This was a relief, as it meant that he probably wouldn't waste too much time trying to 'wind her up', as he usually did with any new acquaintance. Jeannie had a range of tasks that she asked Peter to perform for her, including making a drink, doing some simple cooking and using the vacuum cleaner.

She worked with him for several sessions before making her final assessment, using a standardised Occupational Therapy assessment called the

Assessment of Motor and Process Skills (AMPS), in September. This was part of a wider assessment that included reports from Lesley and from a Clinical Psychologist. Jeannie also spoke at some length with Hannah and myself and asked us to help her fill in a questionnaire. She said that she thought Pete had another condition besides Down's Syndrome and the questionnaire might help us to pin down what it was. She didn't want to be more specific at that point, knowing that we had been down similar avenues before, only to have an incorrect or inconclusive diagnosis.

After Jeannie had been coming to see Pete for a few weeks, we told him that he had been offered a place at the John Gaffney Home, which would be available during the summer holidays. He was non-committal about this but we arranged for him to go for another visit, when he was shown the room that he would occupy and was introduced to the people who would be his flat mates, one of whom he already knew slightly.

We tried not to harp on about it constantly but we did want him to realise that the move was going to happen. I took him to buy a bed and curtains, which he seemed to enjoy, happily telling people that they were for his new bedroom in his new flat.

Otherwise, life carried on as normal. Pete and I had started to collect Neil Taffs' daughter, Frances, from school on a Monday afternoon as her mum had been in hospital and was temporarily unable to drive. Frances also has Down's syndrome but, unlike Pete, was able to attend the local mainstream school where she was making great progress.

Frances and Pete are both strong-minded people and neither of them would give in on any point, so I often had to listen to some lengthy arguments in the car. Our usual routine was to call at the library in Shipley for Pete to borrow a video and then we would go to a café for a drink and a piece of cake. Occasionally, we would call to see Gran and Grandpa at their flat, although if Pete and Frances were particularly argumentative I didn't always inflict that upon them!

Pete had another week's work experience at the Little Chef, this time earning a 50p tip and receiving two C.D.'s from the manager. He was very proud of himself and, once again, we were pleased that things had gone without a hitch.

Some silly behaviour did start to creep in at college, though, which we thought might be a signal that he was worrying about moving into the flat. He was once again eating huge amounts of food at college and drinking far too many cans of fizzy pop. The staff were concerned that he had started to ignore them if he didn't feel like responding to their requests. Although he didn't do anything too terrible, we felt as though we were treading on eggshells, waiting for him to misbehave.

Pete had needed to shave from a fairly early age, being both dark and fairly hairy (despite what he considered to be a rather disappointing array on his chest). Initially, Andy or I had assisted him with this but after we bought him an electric shaver he would usually shave himself and generally managed well. But when he came downstairs one morning to join us at the breakfast table, Hannah and I both stared at him, aghast.

"Pete, what on earth have you done?" we chorused.

"I just wanted to make myself look tidy, so I shaved my eyebrows off," he replied.

What actually possessed him to do it we will never know, but I think he must have received a bit of teasing about it from his pals at college, as he didn't do it again.

In May 2001, we had a bit of a diversion when Pete's cousin Andrew and his wife Lisa, announced the birth of their baby daughter, Emily, ten weeks earlier than scheduled. Weighing in at only 2 pounds 14 ounces, we were all fearful for her survival and rushed to the Clarendon Wing of Leeds General Infirmary, where we peered at the tiny doll-like figure who, nevertheless, already showed signs of a strong, determined character.

Pete was very concerned about her and came with me to visit her on several occasions, before she was finally allowed home some weeks later, having gained sufficient weight. When he was eventually allowed to hold her, he was very gentle and very careful to support her tiny head. Having always shown great tenderness to anyone who he considers to be frail, I knew that he would be very protective towards her

Young Love

Round about this time, Pete announced that he had a new girlfriend called Catherine. After Sarah's appearance at his birthday party, we had seen no more of her, although Pete continued to refer to her as his girlfriend for a time.

Catherine was at college with Peter and they'd been at school together. I took this information with a pinch of salt, suspecting him of making it up, horrible mother that I am. He was fascinated by Hannah's relationship with Tom and I thought that he didn't want to be left out.

It turned out to be true, however, and they were clearly enamoured of each other. When I asked the staff at college about it, they told me that Catherine and Pete sought each other out at break-times and walked hand-in-hand around the campus.

It was difficult for them to arrange to see each other out of college, as Catherine lived in Keighley and neither of them could access public transport, so I thought I would help them. I arranged with Catherine's parents that I would collect her during the spring Bank Holiday so that they could go out somewhere together.

Pete thought that they should go out for lunch, so we settled on a pub we had been to before, in a nice village near Skipton. Pete was very excited at the prospect of taking Catherine out but presumably, because I was there playing gooseberry, they were both painfully shy and hardly said a word to each other. I had taken the newspaper so that they didn't have to talk to me but they were clearly embarrassed. Neither of them ate very much, which was most unlike Pete, at least. However, fortunately, it didn't seem to spoil the friendship, which continued once they were back at college.

Moving Out

We were very proud when Hannah was elected Head Girl of her school, with her responsibilities starting after the May Bank Holiday. Pete was mystified by this and had difficulty in understanding what exactly she was going to do with her 'head'. I'm not sure that he ever did work it out, although we tried to explain her duties to him.

He was much more impressed when she started to learn to drive, having her first lesson on the day of her seventeenth birthday. It wasn't long before he had pestered her into asking the driving instructor if he could go along on one of her lessons. Although I wasn't convinced by this idea, the instructor didn't seem to think it would present any problems. As he pointed out, once she passed her test, she would presumably take Pete out for a drive quite frequently.

My heart was in my mouth when they set off, Pete sitting in the back with a grin stretching from ear to ear. I was terribly anxious until both my 'babies' were safely back home, but they had both clearly enjoyed the experience.

Once Hannah had had seven or eight lessons, I took my courage by the scruff of the neck and let her drive my car. It was nerve-wracking stuff but, again, Pete thought it was great. If she ever stalled the car, he thought it very entertaining. As he sat guffawing in the back I remember thinking, if she can cope with Pete, she can cope with any other unruly passengers.

He never mentioned about wanting to learn to drive himself and presumably saw Hannah as a potential chauffeuse. He seemed to be back to his usual relationship with her since returning home from Weelsby College, and I was hoping that this would continue after he moved into the John Gaffney Home.

Pete moved into his flat in July of that year, after we had arranged for the room to be redecorated and the carpet cleaned, hung his new curtains and put the new bed in place. We bought him a new duvet but let him take his own bed linen from home to add a familiar touch.

We helped him to arrange his ornaments and the pictures he had chosen to take with him, hung his clothes in the wardrobe, then set up his T.V., video and stereo. Although the furniture had seen better days, we were loath to replace it straight away, just in case things didn't work out. I really wanted him to settle there but from past experience, we knew that he would most probably test everybody's patience to the limit.

The John Gaffney Home comprises eight flats, built on two levels, with either two or three residents in each flat. Residents have bedrooms of their own but share a bathroom, kitchen and living/dining room with their flatmates.

To the left of the main entrance is a large lounge that is used for meetings, parties or other social occasions. There is also a laundry room on the ground floor for residents' use, which immediately attracted Pete's interest.

Upstairs, over the entrance, are the offices where the staff are based throughout the day. The residents cover a wide range of ages and disabilities, with some people needing very little support and others needing quite a lot. Assistance can be provided with cooking, budgeting, shopping, cleaning and any other aspects of daily life that residents might find difficult.

At night, one member of staff sleeps in and another is on duty, catching up with paperwork and checking periodically that all is well. If anyone is ill, the other staff member can be called upon for assistance as necessary.

Because the journey to the flat only took us five minutes by car, it was fairly easy to pop in and out to see Pete, thereby making him realise we hadn't abandoned him. He came home to stay for the weekend on a regular basis to begin with and we would often go to his flat for tea.

Driving past his flat twice a day, en route to Hannah's school, was very strange and I had to stop myself from calling in too often but it was reassuring to know that he was so close by. The staff helped us to put on a 'flat-warming' party for him, to which he invited most of the family and several friends. **(Plate 12)**

College restarted at the end of September but he hadn't been back long before the old problem recurred of him spending all his money on sausage sandwiches. This was more problematic than it had previously been, as Pete had less money than before and could not afford to waste it in this way.

Having moved out of the family home, his benefits had changed yet again and he was only receiving the very basic allowances. (It actually took two years for this problem to be sorted out, with us helping him financially during that time.) In order to help him make his money go further, the staff at the home assisted Pete to make sandwiches for his lunch but all that happened was that he ate the sandwiches on the way to college and still spent his money in the canteen.

Apart from that, he seemed to be settling in better than we had dared to hope, with lots of family and friends calling in to visit him or to take him out for a meal. Being physically close to people who were important to him, made a huge difference to Pete. At Weelsby, he had felt isolated, whereas at the John Gaffney Home, he knew that he had friends and family within easy reach.

<u>The Right Diagnosis</u>

One day, a few weeks after he had moved out, I had a phone call from Jeannie McNeil, asking if she might come to see me, as she had some news regarding the questionnaire we had filled in about Pete.

I wasn't sure how I felt when Jeannie arrived – anxious, hopeful, doubtful – a whole range of emotions seemed to be swirling about in my body. But I had the strong feeling that, at last, we would have some sort of diagnosis about whatever else Pete had, apart from Down's Syndrome.

For many years I had been conscious that Pete was not like other people with Down's. Yes, he displayed many of the same traits but there were many areas where he was very different and he had certainly never been 'placid'.

Jeannie had picked up my concerns when she had come to assess his needs for living away from home, when I had voiced the fact that my experiences of being a carer were very different in quality to those of many other parents.

As we sat down together at the kitchen table, Jeannie explained to me that she had also noticed certain types of behaviours during her visits, which led her to think that Pete may have a particular condition called Sensory Integrative Dysfunction (SID).

I quote from Jeannie's report: '*Sensory integration is the ability to organise, process and interpret sensory information, to enable us to make an adaptive response. In our daily lives, we experience a variety of sensations –* **tactile**, **vestibular** *(information from receptors in the inner ear on our movement through space and balance),* **proprioceptive** *(information from receptors in the muscles and joints on our body position),* **aural, visual,** **olfactory** *and* **gustatory***. An adaptive response is a skilled behaviour that is appropriate to the given situation and fulfils its intended purpose.*

It is thought that Sensory Integrative Dysfunction is a significant but undetected problem for individuals with developmental disabilities. When their central nervous system fails to integrate sensory information effectively, they may experience common sensations as confusing or distressing. Because of their learning disability, they may have difficulty understanding what they are experiencing and will be unable to communicate this to their

154

carers in a way that the carers readily understand. Their behaviour and responses can be viewed as logical compensations for an underlying problem.'

Jeannie's report goes on to say that there are several different types of SID, with people having one or a combination of them. **Sensory Modulation** is the process whereby the brain facilitates messages to maximise a response and inhibits others to reduce irrelevant activity. **Sensory Modulation Disorder** occurs when the brain is not filtering messages effectively and is manifested in three different ways; either as **hypo-reactivity** to sensory information i.e. disproportional *under-response,* **hyper-reactivity** i.e. disproportional *over-response* **or** responses that fluctuate between the two.

She continues: *Pete's behaviour indicates that he has responses that fluctuate. He is hypersensitive to sensory input….his brain is not filtering out sensory input from the environment that he does not need to be aware of, therefore he is bombarded by sensations. Pete also shows behaviours which indicate he is trying to calm himself by using strategies that organise and simplify the barrage of sensory information he is experiencing. He may also be hypo-reactive to sensory input, which his brain fails to register from the environment, making him unresponsive to some sensations.*

Jeannie went on to say that Pete's ability to regulate how calm or excited he feels would be impaired by the Sensory Modulation Disorder, resulting in him having difficulty in giving the correct amount of attention to others and in remaining emotionally stable. *'The effect of stimuli on the environment is cumulative and he could easily become distressed if this is not controlled. In these circumstances, only a little more stimuli can be far too much. The resulting emotional outburst may appear sudden and unpredictable but is not if the level of stimulation is recognised. Emotional lability is common – the person is enjoying himself one moment and distressed the next.'*

'Pete's hyper-reactivity is indicated by his distractibility. He is acutely aware of sounds and his visual environment and is very sensitive to smells, sometimes with amusing but embarrassing results. He cannot choose to ignore these sensory inputs but is driven to respond, which is very characteristic of a person who is over-registering sensory input. Pete's ability to attend most to the essential aspects of doing a task and not responding to the less essential is affected. This makes learning tasks more difficult but also results in the task becoming easily disorganised, as he puts elements into the task that are quite irrelevant.

'Pete copes with this hyper-reactivity by relying on his day being highly predictable. His questions are often about what is happening next, his anxiety about this being so high that he would rather make something up about what will happen next, than have no answer.

'As a child, Pete disliked the ornaments at home being rearranged and would often put these back in their original positions. By insisting that ornaments were in the same place, he was trying to produce predictability in his visual environment.'

After moving to John Gaffney, Pete removed pictures from the walls, which Jeannie suggested was his way of making his environment visually less complicated. At home, we had pictures on plain walls whereas at John

Gaffney, many of the walls were covered with patterned wallpaper. This behaviour is called **sensory defensiveness** in that Pete tries to protect his nervous system from sensory overloading that creates rising levels of anxiety.

'Pete's history and some of the difficulties he experiences in physically carrying out tasks indicate that he may have problems in discriminating sensory input from his Vestibular and Proprioceptive system….. Pete shows that he may be hypo-reactive in this area. As a child Pete was often to be found using self-stimulatory behaviours in an attempt to provide his body with this input. He would be found squeezed into small places – the tumble dryer, a washing basket or cupboards; he would grind his teeth or bang them with his hand. (He also liked to carry heavy bags around with him and to wear, at times, what seemed like an inappropriate amount of clothing.)

'Pete's passivity at times is understood if it is appreciated that he is having to put effort into movement that we take for granted. It may also explain that he is happier with tasks that accentuate proprioceptive inputs, such as loading or unloading the dishwasher. Tasks that expect a high level of co-ordination from him will present challenges, as will any that expect him to move skilfully through various working positions. He has managed to overcome his difficulty in navigating around obstacles by being very cautious in moving.'

Concluding her report, Jeannie summarised as follows: *'Pete has difficulty in learning new activities common to people with mild to moderate learning disability but this is compounded by his additional difficulties in the ability of his central nervous system to make sense of sensory inputs. This is revealed chiefly by distractibility and poor control of his levels of arousal, which he expresses in disorganised boisterous behaviour, especially involving electrical equipment. He needs highly structured daily living programmes of activities, which are systematically taught. In this way he can maintain both his attention and his emotional well being and control.'*

Jeannie went on to recommend ways of dealing with Pete's behaviour, described ways of teaching him various tasks and suggested activities and jobs that might be suitable for him to try. She also told me that it explained why he had found having his hair and nails cut was such an ordeal for him. She suggested that when we cut his nails, we should squeeze each nail gently but firmly, to concentrate his mind on that one sensation. Cutting his hair needed to be done quickly and firmly, with confidence, as the fluttering sensations of the hair and scissors would be particularly annoying to him.

When I had finished reading her report, I laid it down on the table, put my head in my hands and wept. Poor Jeannie began to apologise, thinking that her report had distressed me. I tried to regain control of myself as quickly as possible, so that I could explain my tears.

"The content of your report hasn't upset me in the way you think, Jeannie," I told her. "It's the relief of finally having someone explain all the things that we've noticed over the years. Having tried and failed to find an explanation for some of the strange things he's done, I'd come to the conclusion that it must be something to do with the way we've brought him up and that we'd got it horribly wrong. I really can't thank you enough for what you've done."

Jeannie's report was passed on to the staff at the John Gaffney Home and we were hopeful that they would take on board the recommendations in it.

Sad Times

Life seemed to be going better for Peter and his confidence was growing when, in November, my mother died very suddenly. Andy and I had taken Hannah to look round Birmingham University, which was one of the places she had applied to go to the following year.

Mum had been admitted to hospital a few days previously suffering from a chest infection but had appeared to be on the mend, having been taken off the intravenous medication. We had taken Peter to see her once or twice and, although she was clearly tired, she had managed to talk to us and seemed brighter, telling us quite definitely that we should continue with our plans to take Hannah to Birmingham.

It was a huge shock, on our return, to find that she had taken a turn for the worse and been moved into the Intensive Care Unit, dying shortly after we arrived at her bedside. Andy and I had gone to the hospital without the children but we agreed that they should be allowed to come to say their goodbyes to Gran, if they wished to do so.

Both of them wanted to see her and the hospital staff were very accommodating, so we made arrangements to go and collect them. Pete was devastated by the loss of his beloved Gran, although he didn't shed any tears. I think I found his grief harder to deal with than my own, knowing how close he had been to her.

As we left the hospital, Pete wanted to know what would happen to Gran and where she would go. I wasn't really thinking too clearly but replied that the staff would look after her until someone came to take her to a special place, called a Chapel of Rest, until it was time for the funeral service. He kept on about it a little more but I probably only gave him vague answers, as my mind was too full to think straight.

He came home to stay with us for a few days, as we knew he would need our support. Actually, I also needed his. He gives the best cuddles in the world and sometimes a hug from Pete is all I need to cheer me up, if I'm feeling down.

The funeral was arranged for the following week. Pete wanted to know exactly what was going to happen, once again questioning us closely about where Gran was. When I repeated that she was at the Chapel of Rest, he asked if he could go to see her. I was somewhat taken aback, as we had never been the type of family who went in for that sort of thing and I had never, until the night of my Mum's death, even seen a dead body.

After a couple of days of relentless questioning from Pete, I decided I would have to take him. Hannah didn't want to go and neither did Andy, so the two of us set off to the funeral parlour.

We were shown into the Chapel of Rest where Mum was laid out, looking very peaceful but not really quite like my Mum. Pete and I stood together quietly, with me trying very hard not to cry but not entirely succeeding.

After standing quietly, looking into the coffin for a few minutes, I suggested to Pete that he might like to give Gran a goodbye kiss. He was clearly happy to comply with this and leaned over to plant a gentle kiss on her forehead. I was once again moved to tears by his tenderness but as I reached for my handkerchief, Pete stood up and said, in a very matter-of-fact voice:

"She's a bit cold, isn't she?"

It was such a typical comment for Pete, that I found myself laughing through my tears and felt sure that Gran would have laughed, too.

I decided not to try to explain where bodies were kept or why they were cold, so after saying my own, brief goodbye, we set off home.

However, I should have known that Pete would want more explanations and sure enough, as we climbed into the car, he began to ask what would happen to Gran next. Thinking on my feet, I explained that Gran would stay in the special box, called a coffin, until the funeral service and that then she would go to Heaven.

"I'll give her another kiss at church," he said, "before she goes to Heaven."

"You won't be able to do that," I replied, "as they'll have put the lid on the coffin by then."

"What!" he said, clearly shocked by this.

"Well...." I hesitated, knowing that whatever I said would be remembered and repeated, "it's to keep Gran safe on the way to Heaven."

Pete seemed to accept this and, although there were many more questions that week, as long as we all stuck to the same story he seemed to be reassured.

A few days later, Aunty Alison called to see us to express her condolences and kindly took Pete out with her for the afternoon. She told us later that Pete had talked a lot about Gran and about the funeral arrangements. Wanting to offer him some comfort, she had told him that Gran would be all right, as she had now gone to Heaven.

Pete looked at her with a surprised expression and replied, quite firmly:

"She hasn't. She's not going until Wednesday!"

Having been assured by Grandpa that he could still go to stay at the flat from time to time and that Grandpa would cook his breakfast of bacon and eggs for him, Pete then asked, "Now that Gran's not here, will you tuck me into bed?" I was worried that he would ask too many awkward questions of my stepfather but Grandpa seemed quite keen to have Pete to stay, although we were all agreed that this shouldn't happen until the New Year, to give everyone chance to settle down.

After the funeral, we tried to get Pete's life back into some sort of order, encouraging him to return to college and pick up his other activities. Two weeks later we had a telephone call to say that my Mum's younger sister Margaret, who had been a very poorly lady for many years, had passed away.

It just seemed too much too deal with, so soon after losing Mum. It was hard to maintain a cheerful front for Pete's sake, although we did try. He had enjoyed visiting Aunty Margaret and Uncle Raymond on a fairly regular basis and, although neither of them had been in good health for a long time, they were always pleased to see him. With his uncanny sense of knowing whether people were really ill or not, he usually behaved well at their house and it was somewhere that we had both enjoyed visiting.

The temptation to bring Pete back to live at home was very strong at that time, as he seemed such a sad young man and I just wanted to try to protect him from the things in life that might hurt him.

Fortunately, Andy is much more sensible and pointed out that we can't possibly do that, so the best way to help Pete is to try to teach him to cope with life as independently as possible. The family rallied round, calling to see him or to take him out and we all tried our best to cheer him up.

We knew that it would take him a long time to come to terms with losing his beloved Gran and that he would need plenty of support. Thankfully, as he was living so close to us, that wasn't too difficult to manage.

Final Chapter

Lesley Latham, Pete's social worker back then, called to see him on a fairly regular basis and reported that he was 'ever the good, courteous host, offering coffee and cake.' He has always enjoyed entertaining people (in every sense of the word) and was always delighted to have a visitor.

Having carefully cut generous slices of coffee cake, made especially for him by Grandma or one of the ladies from Saltaire church, he then went on to make the coffee with which to wash it down. Unfortunately, this usually involved 'overflowing mugs and lots of mopping up', which Lesley would try to prevent by helping or prompting Pete, but as she says, 'the result was always the same!'

Pete loved to chat to Lesley about her car, being concerned that she drove a bigger car than her husband. He wanted reassurance from Lesley that she would occasionally let her husband drive the big car, having always been something of a chauvinist about this. If we ever passed a large car with a woman driver he would usually say, "She's borrowed her husband's car, today, hasn't she?"

Christmas was looming and although none of us really felt in the mood for a big celebration, we knew that we would have to make a bit of effort for Grandpa, as well as for Pete. I have almost no recollection of what we did that year but I do remember that Pete came home to stay for several days, before returning to his flat to be with his friends at John Gaffney, where they were planning to have yet another buffet supper before seeing in the New Year together.

As we pulled into the traffic, having said our goodbyes to Pete, it dawned on me, probably for the first time, that he actually lived there – not just stayed there in between visits home - and that he had a life of his own. I thought back to the days when the idea of him one day living independently from us had seemed like a pipe dream. Although I knew that there would be many challenges ahead for all of us and times when I would still want to run to his rescue, I was also aware that if the apron strings had not exactly been cut, they had been well and truly undone.

The final word deserves to go to Gillian Tarbotton (previously Miss Bebb), who worked with Pete when he was in the nursery at Greenfield School. She was one of the many people I contacted and I was very touched by her reply. After a gap of sixteen years, I was surprised that she could recall enough about Pete to send me anything – that she could remember enough to write a poem about him, I frankly found astonishing!

I remember the first time that I set eyes on Pete,
Cross-legged on the floor – boy, he looked so sweet.
He flopped his head on to one side and gave his cheeky grin,
And instantly, as was his way, my affection he did win.

The months went by and Pete did blossom,
Began to walk, instead of shuffling on his bottom!
When (rarely!) in trouble, his head would go down,
How could I maintain my 'teacher's frown'?

Pete's favourite was the Greenfield minibus,

160

When we went out – the delight, the fuss.
'Minibus, Miss Bebb?' he'd question – the ride would be his treat.
Climbing up the two big steps, to jump eagerly into his seat.

The sweetest thing I recall of Pete, which always makes me smile,
Is of him bounding up to me, in his usual enthusiastic style.
It was back in the nineteen eighties and was my wedding day,
Pete handed me a horseshoe, but was not there to stay.
Oblivious to the big white dress, and to all the fuss,
He only had one question: 'Miss Bebb... Minibus?!!'

And so those years have long passed by, recorded in this book.
I'm sure that all who've known Pete were dying to take a look.
With a supportive and loving family, Pete's life has been the best,
Now that he has grown up, I'm sure they deserve a rest!

Yet, Pete has been a blessing, as I'm sure you'll all agree.
You wouldn't find him in Morrison's on a 'buy one, get one free'!
So, we'll raise a glass to Peter and wish him happiness,
Because with all the joy he's given, he deserves nothing less!!

Yvonne Crabtree October 2007.